Praise for *Lead*

Leading Together *is the best guidance we have to date about how to collaboratively dismantle the wall that has stood between teachers and school administrators for over a century. This is a marvelously accessible book in which collective leadership is discovered through the eyes and voices of teachers and principals.*

—**Joseph F. Murphy, Frank W. Mayborn**
Chair and Associate Dean
Peabody College of Education
Vanderbilt University
Nashville, TN

In his latest book, Leading Together, *teacher educator Jon Eckert does us a great dual service. On the one hand, he helps impale the myth of the superhero educator (principal or teacher) who single-handedly defends students and defeats all problems facing modern schools. At the same time, he thoughtfully examines a spectrum of collaborative leadership styles. The highlight for many readers will be the realization that effective leadership does not have to be (and increasingly, cannot be) uniform or solitary.*

—**Renee Moore, English teacher**
Mississippi Delta Community College
Cleveland, MS

This refreshing book is upbeat in tone, practical in nature, and noble in approach. Principals and teacher leaders will be able to follow Eckert's advice with confidence and assuredly reap the benefits.

—**James W. Guthrie, Professor Emeritus**
Peabody College of Education
Vanderbilt University
Nashville, TN

Leading Together *re-introduces us to the solution that was there all the time: Every teacher and administrator needs to engage fully with leadership, and they need to do it together. The brilliance of this book is that it models the same strategies it promotes; it is underpinned by rigorous research and draws on deep professional experience developed in collaboration with others. We can finally put to rest the expectation that every school principal lead like Winston Churchill and encourage administrators and teachers to share the opportunities of leadership.*

—**Beth Green, Program Director Education**
Regional Editor Canada
International Journal of Christianity and Education
Hamilton, ON Canada

In Leading Together, *Jon Eckert embeds his study in the practical—poignant questions for self-reflection, examples of real leaders doing this difficult work in real schools—and grounds all of it in his own rich leadership experiences. Above all, this book aims to do what all such literature should: support the adults across our education system in best serving all of our students.*

—Jocelyn Pickford, Designer of the Teaching
Ambassador Fellowship
U.S. Department of Education

As a discipline, leadership is one of the most researched, but least understood, concepts in education. From my vantage point as a superintendent, teacher leadership is critically important in improving the quality of the student experience in our schools. This book brought clarity to the role teachers and administrators can play working in partnership to improve schools. Through this work, Dr. Eckert empowers teacher leaders to recognize opportunities to improve their craft and bring about meaningful and sustained school improvement.

—Jeff Schuler, Superintendent of Schools
Community Unit School District 200
Wheaton, IL

Leading Together *paints a rich portrait of school communities that have learned to combine their collective strengths to become greater than the sum of their parts. The stories, insights, and best practices embody the proverb, "If you want to go fast, go alone. If you want to go far, go together." Whether you're a teacher, administrator, policymaker, or anyone else dedicated to the students who are the true purpose of our work, this book will provide practical ideas, probing questions, and plenty of inspiration for how we can go far together.*

—Justin Minkel, Second-Grade Teacher and
2007 Arkansas Teacher of the Year
Jones Elementary
Springdale, AR

Leading Together *includes rich research-based stories, reflective activities to spark action, and optimistic evidence about what this needed shift in school hierarchies means for improving student outcomes. Don't just read this; adopt it as your guidebook to become an even more influential leader.*

—P. Ann Byrd, COO & Partner
Center for Teaching Quality
Carrboro, NC

In this powerful resource Eckert argues that school transformation depends on the systematic development of collective leadership. Through vivid, well-constructed stories, Eckert provides a guide that readers can use to cultivate effective school leadership in their own setting.

—**Mark A. Smylie, Professor Emeritus**
College of Education
University of Illinois at Chicago
Chicago, IL

A transformational dive into what it means to have genuine and powerful leadership in our education system, Leading Together *will help open up dialogue around issues and topics that are paramount to system success. Although these topics are messy and complex, Dr. Eckert tackles them head on and with grace, understanding, and an authentic perspective that will have you wanting to take on the tough job of transforming our schools to better serve our ultimate client, students. As an instructor of preservice educators, I plan to place this on my syllabus as a must read.*

—**Tammie J. Schrader, Computer Science and Science Coordinator**
Northeast Washington Education Service District 101
Spokane, WA

Once again, Jon Eckert offers his straightforward, no-nonsense thinking to busy practitioners. In Leading Together, *he implores readers to think beyond the typical roles and boundaries of leadership in order to improve results for students. His authentic knowledge of everyday life in schools coupled with a thoughtful framework informs every chapter in this book. There are elements of his model that can be used right away...big shifts or little tweaks! His stories and humor make it readable (and meaningful!) for those of us seeking creative and collaborative ways to lead schools and districts.*

—**Joan Dabrowski, Assistant Superintendent for Teaching and Learning**
Wellesley Public Schools
Wellesley, MA

This is the first book that I have read that provides an adaptable solution to building leadership capacity in schools. Readers will be empowered to recapture the profession through shared leadership. Dr. Eckert provides a perfect blend of research, resources, reflective questions, and real-school examples that grabs the readers' interest. If you want to invest in human capital and improve leadership in your school or district, this is the perfect book!

—**Chris Silagi, Principal**
Whittier School
Wheaton, IL

There are few books that promote uplifting the teaching profession like this one. If we desire to improve outcomes for all students and society as a whole, all educators must work together as they develop their leadership side by side and promote the work within the system.

—**Nancy Veatch, Teacher and Principal**
Bend Elementary School
Cottonwood, CA

This is the book that education in our country needs right now. Jon Eckert's professional experiences as a researcher, practitioner, teacher educator, and policy leader help bring a deep and layered view of the complexities of leadership development. The conversation starters are catapults to embrace uncomfortable and bold dialogue among those truly invested in building better systems for student learning. Prepare to be transformed, no matter what role you have in education.

—**Megan M. Allen, NBCT, EdD**
Master of Arts in Teacher Leadership
Mount Holyoke College, Hadley, MA

While many experts are calling for teachers to be leaders, this insightful analysis makes clear the often overlooked role that school and district leaders play in creating the cultural and systems that enable teacher leaders to play meaningful roles in school leadership.

—**Kristan Van Hook, Senior Vice President for Public Policy & Development**
National Institute for Excellence in Teaching
Santa Monica, CA

Leading Together

Teachers and Administrators Improving Student Outcomes

Jonathan Eckert

Foreword by Barnett Berry

CORWIN
A SAGE Publishing Company

FOR INFORMATION:

Corwin

A SAGE Company

2455 Teller Road

Thousand Oaks, California 91320

(800) 233-9936

www.corwin.com

SAGE Publications Ltd.

1 Oliver's Yard

55 City Road

London, EC1Y 1SP

United Kingdom

SAGE Publications India Pvt. Ltd.

B 1/I 1 Mohan Cooperative Industrial Area

Mathura Road, New Delhi 110 044

India

SAGE Publications Asia-Pacific Pte. Ltd.

3 Church Street

#10-04 Samsung Hub

Singapore 049483

Publisher: Arnis Burvikovs

Development Editor: Desirée A. Bartlett

Editorial Assistants: Kaitlyn Irwin and Eliza Riegert

Production Editor: Amy Joy Schroller

Copy Editor: Janet Ford

Typesetter: Hurix Systems Pvt. Ltd.

Proofreader: Annie Lubinsky

Indexer: Amy Murphy

Cover Designer: Candice Harman

Marketing Manager: Nicole Franks

Printed in the United States of America.

Library of Congress Cataloging-in-Publication Data

Names: Eckert, Jonathan, author.

Title: Leading together : teachers and administrators improving student outcomes / Jonathan Eckert.

Description: Thousand Oaks, California : Corwin, [2018] | Includes bibliographical references and index.

Identifiers: LCCN 2017032467 | ISBN 9781506380155 (pbk. : acid-free paper)

Subjects: LCSH: Educational leadership—United States. | Teacher-administrator relationships—United States. | School management and organization—United States. | School improvement programs—United States. | Academic achievement—United States.

Classification: LCC LB2805 .E26 2018 | DDC 371.2—dc23

LC record available at https://lccn.loc.gov/2017032467

This book is printed on acid-free paper.

17 18 19 20 21 10 9 8 7 6 5 4 3 2 1

Contents

*For all of the remarkable teachers and principals I know
who do hard leadership work together*

Foreword

For at least forty years, school reformers have called for some form of teacher leadership in efforts to improve teaching and learning. Think tanks are now calling for leadership from those who teach. State education agencies are setting standards for teacher leaders. Growing numbers of school districts are putting teacher leadership programs in place so more classroom experts can assist in instructional improvement efforts.

Jon Eckert's new book, *Leading Together: Teachers and Administrators Improving Student Outcomes*, could not publish at a more auspicious time. Growing evidence of the relationship between teacher collaboration and student achievement is mounting. For example, John Hattie (2012), in his meta-analyses of over 800 studies, found that *collective teacher efficacy* was by far the most influential school-level variable in improving academic success. Collective teacher efficacy is two times as important as teachers receiving sound feedback—and is most likely to emerge when teachers build mastery in teams and principals know how to support them in doing so (Donohoo & Velasco, 2016).

Jon makes the case, with both professorial erudition and homespun homily, for a form of collective leadership that is less about management training of and the charismatic personalities of leaders, but "the hard *work* that teachers and administrators do with and for students that ultimately benefits our society." He has filled his book with insights from organizational science research as well as down-to-earth case studies of schools and the educators who lead them. In doing so, Jon paints a portrait of "what" and "how" teachers and administrators are leading, and what helps and hinders them in their efforts to lead together. By reading Jon's book, practitioners can begin to learn how to develop leadership for the work that matters most and reorganize schooling that cultivates everyone, including students, as leaders.

In writing *Leading Together*, Jon logged many hours in schools and interviewed teachers of the CTQ Collaboratory as he explored how they developed the agency and the skill to lead in bold ways. As he notes in Chapter 6, "Every one of the teacher leaders interviewed cited administrative support as key to their development." He also noted how their leadership work rested on their "sense of efficacy." Jon makes an important point here about the need to dispense of the all-too-common "lose/win culture around leadership." The ascent of teacher leaders does not mean the descent of principals and their leadership. Research sponsored by the Wallace Foundation puts an exclamation point on this matter: Collective leadership has a stronger influence on student achievement than individual leadership—and administrators do not lose influence when teachers gain it (Seashore-Louis, Leithwood, Wahlstrom, & Anderson, 2010).

Jon's book comes along at a time when teachers and administrators must serve increasing numbers of special needs students (including those living in poverty and whose first language is not English) while also facing deepening cutbacks in public education budgets. His important work emerges just at a time when a new wave of school reform is washing up on educators—one that places a premium on jettisoning the fixed school-based curriculum and moving toward personalized, competency-based, and socio-learning for every student. Jon's portraiture serves as powerful counterfactual to the longstanding images of teachers siloed in their classrooms, and principals holding steadfast to their role as *the* instructional leader. He does so at a time when public educators must play a vital role in ensuring that students are the well-educated citizens our society needs. Democracy demands collective leadership—and so do our public schools.

I am hopeful that the time has come for collective leadership to become a driving force in creating more equitable and excellent learning for students—despite the powerful forces that are at play to privatize our schools and undermine the public good of public education.

Here is why:

- Three in four teachers engage in informal learning.
- Six in ten teachers use technology to find resources and colleagues to assist them in serving students.

- One in three participate in some type of external network outside of their formal school district and charter organizations.
- Three in four principals believe their job is "too complex"—and they are looking for and finding ways to engage with teachers and not just supervise them.

We now know that the public still supports public education—and continues to have trust and confidence in teachers. Imagine if more of them could translate the images and evidence that Jon offers into political action.

Jon's book, with a bounty of exemplars, offers a roadmap for teachers and administrators to take the bold steps needed to organize schools for collective leadership in service of students. With his rich narratives and careful citations of relevant scholarship, *Leading Together* lets us know what collective leadership can look like and what we can do to create more of it. Read. Learn. Share. Lead collectively.

—Barnett Berry, Founder and CEO

Center for Teaching Quality

Preface

I am optimistic about what schools will do in the coming decades. My optimism is grounded in the many classrooms across our country where great teaching occurs every day. Humble, resilient administrators, teachers, and students are doing this work. We just need to spread what is happening so that this work penetrates every classroom.

Leadership is the hard *work* that teachers and administrators do with and for students that ultimately benefits our society. Leadership is what is done, not who is doing it. The work is fluid and context-dependent, which means that the work—not the position, role, or personality—dictates who leads. This work necessarily blurs the lines between teachers and administrators because it is about the work, not the position.

This is good.
This is needed.
The blurring is already happening.

For the past two decades, I have tried to do this work in schools, colleges, and in the U.S. Department of Education. Over the past three years, I also studied leadership development through hundreds of hours of observations, surveys, interviews, and focus groups with hundreds of teachers and administrators in suburban, rural, and urban—and traditional public, charter, and private schools. Mark Smylie, an educational leadership expert, and I developed a model of leadership development to use as a lens to examine schools. The stories are real. They represent challenging realities grounded in a gritty optimism. Rooted in research, this book is a tool for administrators and teachers.

I hope *Leading Together* builds on *The Novice Advantage: Fearless Practice for Every Teacher*, a book that highlights ways that teachers can grow with one another. My intention is that this book will capitalize on that work so that schools can grow in ways that improve student outcomes.

This book represents the hopeful evidence that I found in schools and describes the work that needs to happen to transform all of our schools. It is not a prescription with a few pieces of evidence on how to get better. It is a tool for administrators and teachers to grow together because school leadership is complex and deeply contextualized. Leadership is not synonymous with administration. It is not about the lone, charismatic leader. It is not about the superhuman teacher single-handedly fighting the system. It is about educators (in administration and in teaching) working together to improve student learning.

I know you are busy. I have also taught long enough to know how people read. Feel free to pick and choose chapters most helpful to you given the time you have and your specific needs. If you need to read this in three- to five-minute chunks between meetings or before you fall asleep with your face in the book, you can. If you have more time, there is plenty to digest and a broad literature base to consume. Each chapter is frontloaded with key takeaways and framing questions. Each chapter has discussion questions, action steps, and "what can we do right now?" sections for teachers and administrators. There are reflection boxes embedded in each chapter. Ideally, teachers and administrators will read this together so that they can then lead and learn together.

Chapter 1, Developing Leadership for the Work That Matters Most describes the current opportunities and challenges for developing the leadership schools need.

Chapter 2, The "Ideal" School outlines a model for teacher leadership development derived from research in the organizational sciences for leadership development, work redesign, and teacher leadership. It describes a model, not for a perfect school, but for schools that can become ideal in your diverse contexts.

To ground the ideal in reality, **Chapter 3** to **Chapter 5** offer insights from three different schools: one rural, one urban, and one suburban. For ease of comparison, the schools are all traditional public high schools, but you can apply the lessons to all types of schools; you will find supplements with evidence from all levels. These chapters address issues that affect all schools—federal policy, issues of poverty, English language learning, school safety, and equity. The insights are applicable to all different contexts, but if you are pressed for time, choose your own adventure based on your particular context.

Chapter 3, The Rural Grassroots tells the story of a small, rural school that is allowing the leadership work to bubble up based on the identified needs of students and teachers.

Chapter 4, The Urban Transition details the leadership work that began seven years ago when all thirteen administrators at this large, urban school were fired midway through the year.

Chapter 5, The Suburban Blueprint describes the pervasive and increasing relational trust growing through teacher-administrator collaboration and professional learning communities that support shared leadership work in a large, suburban school.

The final two chapters describe the opportunities, challenges, and next steps that leaders and research suggest.

Chapter 6, Ideal Leaders, Not Solo Superheroes compiles the wisdom of teacher leaders from across the country about what was vital for their development and work in their schools. Their insights, while unique from the evidence collected in schools, point to the need for systemic development of leadership work for school improvement.

Chapter 7, Fearless Improvement describes what schools can do to design work, build capacity, and deliver results for students. This chapter also provides the tools to move the work forward that will transform your school. If you are like me—impatient, pragmatic, and strapped for time—you may be tempted to skip to this chapter. One word of warning: if you do, you will miss some of the powerful insights from leaders doing the leadership work that has to be done. We need to know the stories before the resolution makes any sense.

Acknowledgments

As with anything I write, this book would not be possible without the examples, support, and hard work of others. For over two decades, I have been the beneficiary of amazing colleagues—administrators, teachers, students, and parents. They influence everything I write. For this book, three schools welcomed me into their communities. The Center for Teaching Quality brought together some of the best teachers in the United States and allowed me to spend several days interviewing them and collecting evidence. I am so grateful to these schools and leaders for their honesty and examples.

Through data collection and writing numerous drafts, I had significant help and feedback from many people. At the risk of leaving some people out, I have to specifically thank McKenna Fitzharris, Erin Bagley, Mark Hiben, Jasmine Ulmer, Joan Dabrowski, Barnett Berry, Ann Byrd, and Alesha Daughtrey. Barnett, Ann, and Alesha, thank you for always pushing my thinking, helping me think differently about collective leadership, and for making me part of your work family at CTQ. Mark Smylie, thank you for your mentorship and friendship that started around this leadership development work.

Thanks to my colleagues at Wheaton College, particularly the education department, for giving me the time through my sabbatical to collect evidence in schools. Thanks especially to Patti McDonell, Paul Egeland, Dot Chappell, and Phil Ryken for your constant support and encouragement.

As always, I am grateful for the Corwin team as they guided me through this process—especially Arnis Burvikovs, Desirée Bartlett, and Kaitlyn Irwin.

Finally, my family makes all of this work possible. The providential blessing of my parents, brothers, wife, and children ground me in the reality of what is most important. Thank you, Ben, Sarah, and Grace for being the best kids I could imagine. Carolyn, thank you for always being my first editor, counselor, reality check, and best friend.

About the Author

 **Jonathan Eckert** was a public school teacher outside of Chicago and Nashville for twelve years. He earned his doctorate in education at Vanderbilt University and served as a U.S. Department of Education Teaching Ambassador Fellow in both the Bush and Obama administrations. Currently, he is an associate professor of education at Wheaton College, where he prepares teachers and returns regularly to teach in the district where his career began. In addition to leading professional development across the country, he has published numerous peer-reviewed and practitioner articles on teaching effectiveness and education policy and is the author of *The Novice Advantage: Fearless Practice for Every Teacher* (Corwin, 2016).

CHAPTER 1

Developing Leadership for the Work That Matters Most

Think of a school leader. Who do you see?
A principal?
A teacher?
A charismatic superhero?

I asked a high school department chair how she developed teacher leadership in others. She was so excited to tell me about the luncheons she put on for her teachers, the t-shirts that they had made up each year, as well as her "Don't worry, be happy now" chalkboard. I really appreciated her energy, passion, and her obvious love for students and teachers. Then, she started telling me about how she likes to give teachers "something to feel responsible for." To illustrate, she began describing her "mint officer" and how her department managed their office mints.

> In that top cabinet, I have twenty-five pounds of those little wintergreen mints. I have a mint officer. She sends an email to everyone in the department, and she asks everyone to donate a bag. And then when mints are running low, I email her, and I say, "You gotta be on this."

This kind of thinking that so many people have is indicative of the limited understanding of leadership development. Leadership development is about so much more than task delegation or getting people to "buy in" to ideas.

We don't need more mint officers. We don't need more people to "buy" what other people are selling. We need the collective expertise of administrators, teachers, students, and school communities to bring about real, effective, and positive change. Being a school leader is hard; we need more effective leadership development to accomplish this hard work. For that to happen, administrators and teachers need to lead together. Instead of "many hands make light work," in schools, the motto should be "many hands make the work possible."

The good news is that effective leadership development is happening because teachers and administrators are working side by side to do the work that best serves students. This book is filled with those examples. In order to capture the raw, unvarnished realities in their stories, I promised anonymity to the schools and all research participants. It isn't their names that matter; what matters is the work. Here are four brief glimpses into those stories:

The rural high school: If the principal needs something, he walks across the parking lot to the superintendent who works out of a trailer in the parking lot of the high school. In the spring, teachers and administrators invite student representatives to participate with them in a two-day retreat to write their school improvement plan for the following year. The idea of having students participate in this process grew from a culture that encourages risk, learns from failure, and supports solutions of the people in the school who are the closest to the challenges.

The urban high school: Seven years ago, all thirteen administrators were fired halfway through the year due to poor school performance, but continued in their roles until the end of the school year, taking teacher morale to unimaginable depths. The principal who was tapped to take over the following year, an elementary principal in the district whose own children attended the high school, recognized the challenges the school faced. Over the past seven years, he has successfully built trust with his teachers through their work together on school safety, positive behavior intervention supports, and school culture, and is now tackling classroom practice. Last year they were nationally recognized for creating a positive school culture. Graduation rates and test scores have improved. The school just voted overwhelmingly (84%) for weekly professional learning community meeting times after a similar measure failed to gain traction the previous year. While there is still much leadership work to be done, the school is on the path toward a more collaborative and trusting culture that produces results for students.

The suburban high school: I am observing a professional learning community of chemistry teachers. A special education teacher is examining student work of various at-risk students with two teachers while three others are designing a new lab to use the following week. A first-year teacher is leading the lab design based on his experience as a bench chemist. He is experimenting with the appropriate concentration of a solution as the other teachers record the data for the lab. The teachers are engaged in an inquiry process that is the same process they will use with their students in the coming week. The principal attends all functions—sporting events, concerts, plays, clubs—and tweets about everything.

The large urban district: The district leader spends half his time in the classroom and the other half developing teacher leadership. A self-described "independent thinker" who manages a large following on Twitter and writes for *The Atlantic* and other outlets, he describes the work he has been doing in this hybrid role in the twenty-seventh largest district in the country. He says, "The bureaucracy is massive. There is such a lack of collaboration between teachers and the district office. In order to make things happen, we have to break down some of those barriers. I am starting to move the rudder on the battleship."

These four examples give me hope. My hope is not based on a theoretical model of what could be. I am not wandering around in a fog of ignorant, academic naiveté. This hope is rooted in the uncompromising reality of what these schools, administrators, and teachers are doing each day. They have a tenacious optimism based on what they have done and continue to do in their schools. With that gritty optimism comes humility. None of the educators I interviewed or observed believe they have everything figured out; they know that context matters and that there is not one right way to develop the leadership needed to spread the good work that they and their students are doing.

Whether you are a school leader in a traditional public, charter, or private school, your gritty optimism is grounded in the humility that grows from the understanding that there are no easy answers. You need to find context-specific solutions. If you are in a private school, you probably won't have a district office, but you certainly have a board and group of parent constituents with strong opinions. Throughout this book, you can insert "parents/board" for district office and you will be able to identify key ideas for developing leadership.

WHAT WOULD IT TAKE TO REALLY TRANSFORM SCHOOLS?

Leadership work should transform schools. We throw the word "transform" around very loosely. It sounds very active, almost magical, and just out of reach. So, what does it really mean?

To better understand what the word means, a colleague pointed me toward an unlikely source, Michael Pollan's book *Cooked: A Natural History of Transformation* (2013). Cooking transforms food, both literally and figuratively. He writes, "Even the most ordinary dish follows a satisfying arc of transformation, magically *becoming something more than the sum of its ordinary parts*" (p. 4).

Transformation changes the essential qualities of something. Food becomes more easily digestible, safer, and the cause for communal gathering through service to each other. How does this apply to schools? Leadership development should change the essential qualities of the school so that its sum is greater than its parts. This is what it means to transform schools in a positive way. Transformation does not necessarily imply that a school is moving from "bad" to "good." A school that is transforming is one that is becoming more than the sum of its parts. In this sense, every school can be continually transformed. However, this process must occur in a disciplined way, not in a haphazard hodgepodge of annual, monthly, or even weekly initiatives (Collins & Hansen, 2011).

For a school to become more than the sum of its parts, leadership must be collective. Schools must tap into skills, abilities, and even collective intelligence that research has shown to be more than the average of individual intelligence (Woolley, Chabris, Pentland, Hashmi, & Malone, 2010). The performance of humans across a range of different kinds of cognitive tasks has been encapsulated as a common statistical factor called g or general intelligence factor. What intelligence actually is, is unclear and hotly debated, yet there is a reproducible association of g with performance outcomes, such as income and academic achievement (Woolley et al., 2010). Collective leadership encompasses the practices through which teachers and administrators influence colleagues, policymakers, and others to improve teaching and learning.

> *Collective leadership encompasses the practices through which teachers and administrators influence colleagues, policymakers, and others to improve teaching and learning.*

In order to explore what is really happening in schools in different contexts, I used the University of Chicago's 5Essentials Survey (2016) that is administered to all schools in the state of Illinois. The survey measures organizational changes and predicts probability for school success (see sidebar). I was interested in how teacher leadership was being developed in high schools because of their size and complexity. They are also at the end of the P-12 system and therefore inform and are informed by the entire system. Having spent most of my professional life in middle and elementary schools, these high schools provide an outstanding lens for reflecting on leadership at those levels. I was also interested to know how the challenges of a high school were different depending on whether it was located within an urban, suburban, or rural context. To find out, I decided to take a deep dive into schools in one of the most challenging states in the country to determine how teacher leadership could be developed: Illinois.

1.1 WHAT CAN WE DO RIGHT NOW?

Being a school leader is hard work and time-consuming. Some of this material is hard to read without getting defensive. Throughout the book, there are boxes built in for you to reflect, hopefully with colleagues, administrators, and teachers alike. These breaks should create space for honest, transparent conversations that are free of judgment. They are designed to help you immediately apply what you are reading to your context even if it feels a bit uncomfortable.

If you are a district administrator, you might chafe at the way a teacher characterized district leadership as an impediment to improvement. If you are a school administrator, you might take offense at the notion that teachers do not always trust you. If you are a teacher, you might be bothered by the insinuation that you do not understand all of the challenges that school and district administrators face. If you find yourself getting defensive, then that is the time to really pay attention.

- Is your school benefitting from collective leadership?
- When was the last time teachers and administrators in your school participated in professional learning together (not administrators checking in, but actually learning together)?

- What would professional learning that engaged both administrators and teachers look like?

From a state policy perspective, there may be no state more challenging than Illinois. The state has the largest funding disparity between low and high poverty districts in the United States (four to one). In addition to a pending pension crisis and budget strife between a governor and legislature, the state's credit rating is the worst in the nation (and still sinking), and Illinois faces the challenges of having 852 different school districts with a state department of education that has lost 60 percent of its staff since

The 5Essentials survey (University of Chicago, 2016) reliably measures organizational changes and indicates probability for school success around five key factors.

1. *Effective leaders:* The principal works with teachers to implement a shared vision.

2. *Collaborative teachers:* Teachers work together in order to promote professional growth.

3. *Involved families:* The entire school staff attempts to build external relationships connected to the school.

4. *Supportive environments:* The school is safe and supportive of students, teachers, and families.

5. *Ambitious instruction:* Teachers are clear, engaging, and academically challenging.

Schools that are strong on the five essentials are five times more likely to improve student learning than schools weak on the five essentials. To find the high schools around which to develop case studies, I was particularly interested in the first two factors: *effective leaders* and *collaborative teachers*. I selected schools that had a minimum average implementation rating for effective leadership and collaborative teachers, which is the middle rating of the five-tiered rating system. Using publicly available demographic data (Illinois State Board of Education, 2016), I identified one urban, one suburban, and one rural school.

2007. Certainly, other states have their own challenges, but that is the point: collective leadership can be developed anywhere.

WHY LEADER*SHIP*, NOT JUST LEADER?

The focus of this book is leadership development, not leader development. Research shows that teachers (Hanushek, 1992; Rivkin, Hanushek, & Kain, 2005; Sanders & Rivers, 1996) and principals (Branch, Hanushek, & Rivkin, 2012; Grissom, Kalogrides, & Loeb, 2015; Leithwood, Seashore-Louis, Anderson, & Wahlstrom, 2004) are the two greatest school-level factors impacting student learning.

We also know that systems matter. Improvement is about more than one individual. "A bad system beats a good person every time" (Deming, 1993).

Both teachers and administrators are important.

Both are leaders.

Collective leadership matters (Seashore-Louis, Leithwood, Wahlstrom, & Anderson, 2010).

Educators spend too much time down in the weeds worrying: *Who is a leader? Who is not a leader? Is a leader defined by a position?* Many times, these conversations are driven by contracts and collective bargaining language that separates teachers and administrators. These can be important questions, but they are not the questions that will actually improve education. One of the primary attributes of great school leaders—both administrators and teachers—is the fact that they don't define, they do. They get things done.

Leadership is the *work* (not individuals, personalities, or roles) that drives an organization's mission. Leadership is composed of functions, not roles (Firestone, 1996). Just as research has shown the benefit of focusing on teaching instead of the teacher (Hiebert & Stigler, 2017), we must focus on leadership instead of the leader. Of course, leadership does not occur without relationships and influence, but if we view leadership as work, then this makes development fluid and competency based. We develop leadership by doing the work required to move the school forward. The "what" of the leadership work determines "who" should be developed and how their development should occur.

Here are a few clarifications and propositions about leadership. First, leadership is not intrinsically good—its goodness is contingent on the organization's mission (Smylie & Mayoretz, 2009). There are many schools that have strong and forceful leaders, but this does not mean that their leadership is in the best interest of students.

Second, leadership is contingent on followership—influence matters. No one leads without followers; therefore, developing followers is part of developing leaders. I have personally experienced, and also found in my research, many instances where leaders were developed only to return to schools where no one was interested in following them. This is a major issue for both the aspiring leader and the disinterested followers. The leader has new insights and a desire to spread influence to others, and yet no one wants to listen. As a Vanderbilt professor of mine liked to say, "Insight without action breeds cynicism." Leadership is not about superheroes, but cynicism is cultural kryptonite for leadership.

We need strong leadership *from* teachers, not leadership *of* teachers. Our schools should be teacher-powered, not teacher-proofed. For collective leadership to flourish, we need leadership from administrators—leadership that is strong enough to support the school's mission, much of which has to be led by teachers.

Leadership requires hard work. I can think of no better examples of leadership through hard work than Orville and Wilbur Wright. The courage, intelligence, and ingenuity that the brothers needed to invent the first airplane might be obvious. However, the characteristic that might have been the most essential for their success was their work ethic. They even impressed people who presumably were very difficult to impress: the inhabitants of the Outer Banks of North Carolina at the turn of the twentieth century. This was a place inaccessible by road and at the mercy of shifting sands and the Atlantic Ocean. One of the few residents of Kitty Hawk, North Carolina, described the Wrights as "two of the workingest boys" ever seen, "and when they worked, *they*

1.2 WHAT CAN WE DO RIGHT NOW?

What would happen in our school if we stopped using "transform" and "teacher leadership" generically?

Is leadership more about the leader or the work? Place an "x" on the spectrum line below. Where would you place leadership?

Leader_____Work

How does where you place your "x" on the line above affect your willingness to lead?

worked.... They had their whole heart and soul in what they were doing" (McCullough, 2015, p. 54). I am not suggesting that educators just need to work harder. I am suggesting that the leadership work they need to choose is the type that engages their whole heart and soul—what Angela Duckworth refers to as "passion and perseverance" (2016).

Patric Lencioni describes the ideal team player as someone who is humble, hungry, and socially intelligent (Lencioni, 2016). Being humble, hungry, and socially intelligent are characteristics of an individual. Do the Wright brothers fit this description? The Wright brothers were certainly humble and hungry. Wilbur describes his drive toward long-term goals this way: "A man who works for the immediate present and its immediate rewards is nothing but a fool" (McCullough, 2015, p. 246). He definitely took the long view of leadership. The Wrights demonstrated social intelligence in their work with one another and were a legendary team nearly free of ego.

Are we now talking about leaders instead of leadership?

I don't think so. Like so many amazing educators, the Wright brothers exemplify what leadership really is: work. Most leaders I know are not charismatic forces of nature. They are simply doing the leadership work that needs to be done. In interviews with nationally identified teacher leaders, I posed the question: "Is leadership more about the person or the work?" Fourteen out of fifteen leaders said it was about the work. Most did not even hesitate and many added, "Of course it is about the work—it is about our students." These teachers, like the Wrights, were not trying to be leaders or looking for particular leadership positions. They were just doing the work. In so doing, they developed the skills and knowledge necessary to expand their work; thus, they were expanding their leadership.

Interestingly, when I posed this question to teachers and administrators in the three high schools in Illinois, less than 50 percent of them identified leadership as being about the work. However, the teachers and administrators who did identify leadership as being more about the work had more evidence of impact and influence than did their colleagues who saw leadership as being more about the person. Viewing leadership as being about the work instead of the individual, position, or personal characteristics seems to be liberating and empowering. Educators seem more likely to do the leadership work that best serves their students when they are focused on the work and not their own inadequacy or the limitations of a position. Clearly, both the person and the work are important, but does it change your willingness to lead if you view leadership as being about the work more than the individual?

If leadership is not about you, does that alleviate your concerns about your inadequacies? It should. We just need to get to work.

1.3 WHAT CAN WE DO RIGHT NOW?

If we are interested in leader*ship* as work, understand that leadership is not intrinsically good, and understand that leadership *and* followership must be developed, then the following four propositions are essential:

Proposition #1: A school's mission is to improve outcomes for society through students.

Proposition #2: Based on this mission, much of the leadership work of a school must necessarily be performed by teachers.

Proposition #3: Leadership and followership should be developed thoughtfully and systematically.

Proposition #4: Leadership *development* most effectively occurs when students, teachers, and administrators lead and learn side by side as they seek to advance and refine the school's mission.

What do you think: Are our schools designed for this type of collective leadership?

Who is following you?

Who are you following?

Do leaders and followers in your building change based on the leadership work that is occurring?

WHY COLLECTIVE LEADERSHIP, NOT TEACHER LEADERSHIP OR ADMINISTRATIVE LEADERSHIP?

Sometimes we treat school leadership as if it is synonymous with administrative leadership.

This is a mistake.

Administrative leadership ≠ school leadership

Administrative + teacher leadership = school leadership

Successful administrators know these two equations. In fact, these administrators are absolutely essential to creating the conditions of the second equation.

Certainly administrative leadership is essential for effective schools (Day, Gu, & Sammons, 2016; Leithwood & Mascall, 2008; Leithwood et al., 2004; Seashore-Louis et al., 2010). Unfortunately, many administrators "are frequently left to lead and learn in isolation" (School Leaders Network, 2014). However, if leadership is about the work that is done in the service of organizational goals, then teacher leadership alongside administrative leadership is essential for that work within schools. Administrators are not isolated if they are learning alongside teachers. Administrators are not isolated if they are learning from teachers and teachers are learning from them in a reciprocal relationship.

My definition of teacher leadership, which is the basis of collective leadership, builds on the work of York-Barr and Duke (2004): Teacher leadership encompasses the practices through which teachers—individually or collectively—influence colleagues, principals, policymakers, and others to improve teaching and learning (Eckert, Ulmer, Khatchatryan, & Ledesma, 2016).

Much has been written about teacher leadership: what it is, what it isn't, how we can get more of it, and why it is good (Katzenmeyer & Moller, 2009; Lieberman & Miller, 2004; Mangin & Stoelinga, 2008; Murphy, 2005; Smylie, Conley, & Marks, 2002; Wenner & Campbell, 2017; York-Barr & Duke, 2004). My purpose is not to rehash this research. If we can stipulate that teacher leadership is about the *work* done to advance the mission of schools, then the question that remains is: How can this kind of leadership flourish?

The complexities of the current educational landscape can all be addressed by the leadership work that teachers and administrators perform together through their students in the service of society. I am not oversimplifying a solution because there are many solutions—not one silver bullet for this challenge, but many. This is "equifinality"—many ways to reach the same goal (Burke, 2014).

Because of the complexity, I hesitate to separate teacher leadership and administrative leadership, but this is so often how leadership is delineated. There are many good reasons for doing this from a contractual and supervisory perspective, but for the purposes of leadership development, the lines really should be blurred. In fact, this is what is happening at the rural high school I previously described, where teachers, administrators, and students are designing the School Improvement Plan. In this case, the leadership equation looks like this:

Administrator + teacher + student leadership = collective school leadership

and this is the formula for collective school leadership that is most needed.

1.4 WHAT CAN WE DO RIGHT NOW?

Circle the equation that best represents your school's leadership equation:

Administrator leadership = school leadership

Administrator + teacher leadership = school leadership

Administrator + teacher + student leadership = school leadership

What are the ramifications of these equations for your school?

How does this change what you do tomorrow?

(Continued)

(Continued)

How often do teachers and administrators at your school participate in professional learning?

I know this is not a scientific scale, but it is designed to get you to take a position and think as a team.

On a scale of 1 to 10, how "collective" are any leadership development efforts at your school?

1 = "We have one instructional leader."

10 = "Administrators, teachers, and students are constantly learning and leading together."

| 1 | 2 | 3 | 4 | 5 | 6 | 7 | 8 | 9 | 10 |

The Collective Leadership Inventory is designed to get you and your school thinking about the specific needs required to focus on development. Your success with the inventory is dependent on the degree to which you can be honest. Sometimes leadership is about saying something needs to stop. Sometimes it is about saying yes. Effective leadership should build trust. On the inventory, is there a difference between administrators and teachers? What would students say?

WHY DEVELOPMENT, NOT JUST LEADERSHIP?

Those teachers, students, and administrators at the rural high school are not "being developed" to do leadership work. They are developing their capacity for leadership work by doing the work. So, why not just think about leadership and let development take care of itself?

The reason we must focus on development is that without it, leadership efforts can end up being haphazard and short-sighted. How many schools operate with a few administrators

Collective Leadership Inventory	
What initiatives need to stop, or be significantly revised, at my school?	
What do we need more of at my school?	
What do we need to do to ensure that we build trust among students, teachers, and administrators?	
How can we develop students, teachers, and administrators for this work?	
Rate the following: I am passionate about the leadership work happening at our school.	Strongly Disagree Strongly Agree 1 2 3 4 5 6 7 8 9 10

and teachers working to the point of exhaustion to keep the ship afloat? To address this issue, I ask school leaders (teachers and administrators) three questions:

1. Who are the leaders in this building who do most of the leadership work?

   Regardless of the size of the school, leaders generally identify approximately 10 percent of the educators in the school.

   Then I say:

2. Imagine that all of those leaders left the school. Who would the next group of leaders be?

   Typically, the leaders struggle to identify this next group, but they generally come up with several names.

   Then I ask:

3. What are you doing to develop those leaders?

The light bulb, or maybe more like a flashing red light and siren, goes off. Rarely has a school leader been able to tell me what is being done to develop those leaders.

This is a problem on many levels. First, the current leaders are probably stretched too thin. They are acutely aware of the immediate needs of their students such that they cannot address the broader issues facing their schools and districts. They are exhausted by the tyranny of the urgent needs of those students. Additionally, they are trying to make things better with their own innovative ideas that often compete with the ideas coming from the top down. I hear the phrase, "Beating my head against the wall," fairly frequently when leaders describe what they are trying to do.

Second, Katzenmeyer and Moller describe teacher leadership as the sleeping giant that has the potential to transform schools, but believe that the "sleeping giant" of teacher leadership is not being awakened (Katzenmeyer & Moller, 2009). I agree. In almost every school I visited or studied, there is untapped potential for teacher leadership. For a variety of reasons, some teachers do not see the work beyond their classrooms as within their purview. They may be victims of the tyranny of the urgent needs of their students. They may not have a vision of what their leadership could look like. They may lack supportive administration. Whatever the reason, there are teachers who are interested in expanding their work beyond their classrooms.

Third, it is not possible for 10 percent of an organization to do the necessary leadership work to meet organizational goals. If we believe that leadership is about the work that must be done to meet those goals, then the work should dictate the necessary leadership. Leaders' roles and positions are fluid and

Over half of teachers (51%) are at least somewhat interested in teaching in the classroom parttime combined with other roles or responsibilities in their school or district, including 23% who are extremely or very interested in this option (MetLife, 2013, p. 5).

based on the expertise and capacity of those in the organization. The same leaders cannot always lead because the work dictates that different types of expertise are needed for different types of leadership. For example, a principal at a comprehensive high school can create a supportive context for professional learning communities (PLCs), but the leadership essential to make those PLCs work resides within the teachers in different departments. Therefore, ideas for how to improve PLCs should come from the teachers who lead and then open opportunities to share with others.

Leadership development, more than just leadership, is essential for catalyzing and sustaining school improvement. In the next chapter, we explore in more detail what a model of leadership development can look like—a model that considers vision and strategy for leadership development, work design, school conditions, capacity of administrators and teachers, and support.

1.5 WHAT CAN WE DO RIGHT NOW?

List the leaders in your school (i.e., who does the work that drives your school forward—think of "out front" leaders, leaders who are "behind the scenes," and the "glue" people that hold everyone together?).

What is being done to develop these leaders?

If those leaders were gone, who would step into the leadership vacuum?

What is being done to develop those next leaders?

WHAT DO SCHOOLS NEED?

Before we get to the model, we need to briefly address what schools need. More is demanded of schools now than at any point in history. Schools must meet economic, social, emotional, academic, and physical demands for each student—sometimes with fewer resources.

At the same time, we know more now about how people learn than at any point in history (Bransford, Brown, Cocking, & National Research Council, 2000; Hattie, 2009; Hattie & Yates, 2014; Willingham, 2009). We have known for a long time that teachers are the single most important school-level factor that affects student learning (Hanushek, 1992; Rivkin et al., 2005; Sanders & Rivers, 1996). With the 2015 passage of the *Every Student Succeeds Act* (ESSA), states and districts now have more flexibility in how to support and assess teaching and learning. The educational landscape is shifting toward personalized learning, technology integration, and twenty-first century skills.

These are exciting opportunities, but educators are scrambling to keep up. To capitalize on these opportunities and meet the needs of today's students, collective leadership must be a priority. In so many places, it simply is not. We know that trust is essential in any organization (Lencioni, 2002), and particularly in schools (Bryk & Schneider, 2002). However, decades of standards-based reform, test-based accountability, and contentious labor dynamics have eroded that trust (Goldstein, 2014). That trust needs to be deliberately developed.

1.6 WHAT CAN WE DO RIGHT NOW?

Four archetypes from my research capture many of the reasons teacher leadership does not work and are evidence of the lack of development. If you have spent any time in schools, you know these stereotypical profiles:

The Mint Officers: No idea what leadership really is
Work is delegated to them, and then they are micromanaged.

The Anointed Ones: No thought of followership

Principal says they are leaders. No one else agrees.

The Superhumans: No consideration of sustainability

They just keep getting more and more added to their plates until they achieve a career supernova of unbelievable success or they burn out.

The Invisible "Just-A-Teachers": No opportunity for development

When asked if they are school leaders, they reply, "No, I am Just-A-Teacher." This statement is almost a proper noun because it communicates so much.

Here is what I think schools need:

School Leaders: Leadership is developed and enacted based on work

The school leader is an administrator or teacher who works alongside others based on their skills and knowledge to do the work that best serves students.

What type of leader are you?

What type of leader populates your school?

How do we develop more school leaders?

Professional Capital

One way to build that essential trust is through the development of professional capital. Andy Hargreaves and Michael Fullan (Hargreaves & Fullan, 2012) describe four possible roads we might travel. The first three are all dead-end policies, and interestingly, all three likely erode trust. The first is being tried in multiple states and districts in the United States—"a flat-out assault on teachers' pensions and security" (p. xii). The second practice is paying teachers according to individual performance as measured by their students' test scores. The third system is to reduce teaching to a technical reproduction model that diminishes teachers' judgment and professionalism so that less qualified people can teach.

The fourth way, and the only way to long-lasting success, is the development of professional capital, which is composed of human capital, social capital, and decisional capital. In essence, Hargreaves and Fullan argue that we get better together through transparent practice, collection of evidence and personal judgment, and collective responsibility coupled with collective accountability.

Networked Improvement Communities

Tony Bryk and his colleagues at the Carnegie Foundation (Bryk, Gomez, Grunow, & LeMahieu, 2015) have taken this one step further with networked improvement communities (NICs). Building on the lessons learned from the improvement sciences, they suggest systematically collecting evidence of what does and does not work and sharing those data between organizations committed to improvement. The impetus for data collection is not accountability, but improvement. To put it in school terms— systematically collecting formative rather than summative assessment. This orientation toward improvement is all about systematic development.

Building on this work, it is clear to me that schools require reciprocal leadership development. No longer should schools have a lone instructional leader. In a comprehensive high school with departments ranging from performing arts to English to world languages to science, that is a ludicrous idea. A school's orientation should be toward improvement, not overly simplistic accountability; this happens when teachers and administrators work together.

Recently, I talked to a fourth-year teacher working in a charter school who described the "leadership team" at her school. The "team" makes the decisions on curriculum, behavior policies, and classroom structures—including moving first graders through at least six teachers every day. They are trying out bold ideas that may or may not work. However, there are at least three glaring problems with this model:

1. They do not appear to be collecting evidence in a transparent way about how their innovations are working.

2. They are not part of a network of schools where evidence of impact is shared.

3. Most importantly, no teachers are on the "leadership team."

A "leadership team" is only developed in a place of mutual respect. The best way to develop mutual respect is through administrators and teachers creating opportunities and identifying and performing leadership work together. Administrators who keep a foot in the classroom (e.g., possibly co-teaching with a first-grade teacher to see how six class rotations a day might affect a six-year-old, or a teacher working with administrators on constructing a schedule that accommodates the needs of everyone) create powerful opportunities for development.

Disruptive Engagement

What we really need is disruptive engagement. This is Brené Brown's term. She is a researcher and best-selling author on vulnerability. She writes, "To reignite creativity, innovation, and learning, leaders must re-humanize education and work" (2012, p. 187). What does it mean to re-humanize education? The answer is simple, but it is contingent on trust, which is complex. Principals do not develop teachers. Teachers do not develop principals. Development cannot be done to someone. Development occurs *with* one another. Educators develop by working side by side as they engage meaningful work in meaningful relationships. Brown's research has shown that this level of trust and vulnerability is hard to find in schools. Teaching and learning are quite possibly the most human enterprises that we undertake. They are at the core of who we are as human beings. Learning is vulnerable and fragile. Leading learning, therefore, requires a large measure of vulnerability, which is contingent on trust.

Chapters 2 through 6 of this book explore how leadership can be developed to better serve educators so they can better serve students. Together, we explore the implications of research on teacher leadership, work redesign, and leadership development with three real-world case studies and insights from some of the best educators in the United States. In the final chapter, we identify the necessary next steps to re-humanize our work through disruptive engagement. I promise, the steps do not include top-down mandates cloaked as PLCs, micromanagement, or mint officers.

One last caveat—my last book, *The Novice Advantage: Fearless Practice for Every Teacher* (Eckert, 2016), had a number of humorous anecdotes about my need for growth in the classroom. This book is a little different. It is hard to write a book about leadership in schools that is humorous; rather, the anecdotes here are meant to be provocative. I hope this book helps you think through the realities of your own school and that you find the examples meaningful. Similar to *The Novice Advantage,* I am sharing the stories of others so we can reflect, risk, and revise our thinking together in order to better serve each other and our students.

Chapter Review: What Matters Most in Schools (and in This Chapter)?

❖ Leadership is the *work* (not individuals, personalities, or roles) that drives an organization's mission. Leaders do not define, they do.

❖ Leadership development should be collective in order to change the essential qualities of the school so that its sum is greater than its parts.

❖ Collective leadership encompasses the practices through which teachers and administrators— individually or collectively—influence colleagues, policymakers, and others to improve teaching and learning.

❖ Leadership is not intrinsically good—its goodness is contingent on the organization's mission.

❖ Leadership is dependent on followership—influence matters. No one leads without followers, so developing followers is part of developing leaders.

❖ We need strong leadership *from* teachers, not *of* teachers. Teacher-powered, not teacher-proofed. For teacher leadership to flourish, we need administrator leadership.

❖ Teachers and administrators who identified leadership as being more about the work had more evidence of impact and influence than their colleagues who saw leadership as more about the person.

❖ Collective leadership development, more than just leadership, is essential for catalyzing and sustaining school improvement.

❖ Trust is essential for school improvement. We can leverage trust to develop professional capital and networked improvement communities.

❖ We need to re-humanize education through disruptive engagement.

Action Steps

Look back over the six "What can we do right now?" boxes and the Collective Leadership Inventory listed throughout the chapter. If you started to answer those questions with your colleagues, you are well on your way to the leadership work that your school needs.

On a scale of 1 to 10, how well does your school develop collective leadership?

1 = "We trust the U.S. Secretary of Education to tell us what to do."

10 = "Every educator in the building is being developed as a leader based on his or her passions."

| 1 | 2 | 3 | 4 | 5 | 6 | 7 | 8 | 9 | 10 |

1. Does your school or district operate as if leadership is about the work, the position, or the person?

2. How has your leadership been developed? How are you developing leadership with others? Are you developing mint officers or collective leadership?

3. What needs to happen in your school for collective leadership development to occur?

4. What are the obstacles to that development?

5. For administrators: What can I do in the coming week with teachers to develop collective leadership?

6. For teachers: What can I do in the coming week with administrators to develop collective leadership?

7. What does a transformed school look like in your context?

8. How can you engage students in that transformation?

– –

CHAPTER 2

The "Ideal" School

"Design your ideal school."

How many of us have had that assignment in an education class? I am sure at some point I designed a school that was amazing for every learner.... with a $157,000 per pupil price tag—just a slight increase from the average U.S. per pupil expenditure of approximately $11,600.

This can be an entertaining and even helpful thought exercise; however, this does not get us very far down the road of actually improving schools. In the end, designing a theoretical school for a hypothetical context generally consists of designing physical structures, technology, teacher-student ratios, and curriculum that might or might not address the needs of each student. The fact is we need schools that are able to adapt to the ever-changing needs of students and the rapidly accelerating rate of change in education. Consequently, enter the recent calls for teacher leadership as a panacea for nearly every challenge in education (Curtis, 2013; Duncan, 2014; Pennington, 2013):

- Principals are stretched too thin: teacher leadership
- Increased documentation and record keeping for everything: teacher leadership

- Student learning outcomes are lagging: teacher leadership
- Teachers need more instructional support: teacher leadership
- District administrators want to implement a new initiative: teacher leadership
- PLCs should better support teaching and learning: teacher leadership
- ESSA provides additional flexibility for assessment: teacher leadership
- English learners need more support: teacher leadership
- Bullying and discipline issues are increasing: teacher leadership

You and I can continue with example after example of challenges where teacher leadership has become the remedy as if it will just bubble up and miraculously solve all obstacles before you can say, *Freedom Writers, Dead Poet's Society,* and *Dangerous Minds.* In fact, this approach is not very different than dreaming up our ideal schools. There is far more to the solution. As more and more policymakers see teacher leadership as a panacea, more and more evidence of impact will be required. If collective leadership development of administrators and teachers does not occur in a systematic and thoughtful way, how can we expect researchers to find evidence of impact?

NO EASY ANSWERS

We know there are no easy answers. So often, easy answers are the reason for so much skepticism among educators when the next silver bullet appears. Ronald Heifetz (1998), a leadership expert from Harvard, describes what happens so often in organizations, and I would add, particularly in education. We apply technical solutions to adaptive challenges. Adaptive challenges require shifts in mindset (e.g., improved student learning). When we apply technical solutions (e.g., more standardized testing), we do not address the adaptive nature of the challenge. Failure, skepticism, and frustration ensue.

Teacher leadership can be a technical solution. Creating teacher leadership positions, encouraging PLCs, or giving teachers time to observe each other can all be useful. But if they do not address the adaptive nature of the challenge of transforming schools to improve student learning, then they will not get us very far.

This chapter is a combination of research from three bodies of literature and evidence I collected from the three high schools and interviews with school leaders from across the United States. The research comes from the organizational science literature on work design (e.g., Campion, Mumford, Morgeson, & Nahrgang, 2005; Hackman & Oldham, 1980; Humphrey, Nahrgang, & Morgeson, 2007) and leadership development across sectors (e.g., Avolio, 2010; Conger, 1992; Day, Zaccaro, & Halpin, 2004; Fulmer, 1997; Van Velsor, McCauley, & Ruderman, 2010; Yukl, 2013). By joining this research with the research on teacher leadership that has emerged since the mid-1980s (e.g., Murphy, 2005; Wenner & Campbell, 2017; York-Barr & Duke, 2004), there is potential for an adaptive solution. This solution is a model of collective leadership development essential to any ideal school—a school that we cannot fully imagine. I have, however, caught glimpses of what this school model can look like through observations, interviews, and evidence that comprise the next four chapters.

To understand what schools and collective leadership teams can look like, it can be useful to look to innovative examples beyond education. When you think of innovative organizations, which ones come to mind?

Google was possibly one of the names that popped into your head. Interestingly, the company has been studying effective teams for years and found that "who is on a team matters less than how the team members interact, structure their work, and view their contributions" (Rozovsky, 2015). It found five dynamics that matter most for successful teams.

1. Psychological safety: Can we take risks on this team without feeling insecure or embarrassed?

2. Dependability: Can we count on each other to do high-quality work on time?

3. Structure and clarity: Are goals, roles, and execution plans on our team clear?

4. Meaning of work: Are we working on something that is personally important for each of us?

5. Impact of work: Do we fundamentally believe that the work we're doing matters?

Imagine if this was how your school's leadership teams operated. I believe these dynamics apply to effective leadership teams at schools as well. That is why they are all represented in the collective leadership development model that follows.

2.1 WHAT CAN WE DO RIGHT NOW?

Before getting to the model, here is a "Top Twelve" list (a "Top Ten" list was not enough) of what collective leadership development is and is not. There are two to three items that align to five different constructs in the development model and are shaded accordingly. Throughout the remainder of the chapter, there are boxes that provide a bit more context in order to stimulate your thinking on the elements of true leadership development. Hopefully, this fosters some disruptive engagement between teachers and administrators:

	Collective Leadership Development is NOT....	Collective Leadership Development is....
1	Principals getting out of the way	Working side by side
2	Political cover for unpopular decisions	Making the right decisions
3	A formal title	Formal and informal work
4	"Appoint & anoint" or "empower & flower"	The work picking the leader
5	Always instructional	About equity and educational policy
6	Always saying "yes"	Sometimes saying "no"
7	About waiting for permission	Doing what needs to be done
8	Task delegation	Meaningful work toward school goals

9	Pseudo-administration	Boundary spanning
10	More committee work	Flexible work
11	About teacher "buy in"	Shared ownership and expertise
12	Fearful accountability	Fearless improvement

What has been your experience with collective leadership development? Does your experience fall more into the first or second column?

How are the two columns different?

Look for the fearless reflection boxes throughout the chapter for opportunities to further discuss the differences.

In order to give life to the model, I have interspersed glimpses of what it does and does not look like in real schools, by including stories and explanations that describe what collective leadership is and is not. Many of the examples are highlighted in the sidebars. Additionally, I briefly describe each box in the model under a separate subheading.

A COLLECTIVE LEADERSHIP DEVELOPMENT MODEL FOR SCHOOL IMPROVEMENT

When considering individual schools, administrators, particularly principals, are absolutely essential to any collective leadership development efforts. In Figure 2.1, we begin with the principal's development and support for teacher leadership. Of course, all of this occurs within community, district, state, and national contexts that support or constrain the school's efforts, which is why effective district office administrators are so important for bridging and buffering challenges that might impact the school (Durand, Lawson, Wilcox, & Schiller, 2016). At the school level, an effective principal is essential to sustained leadership development.

Figure 2.1   Collective Leadership Development Model for School
Improvement

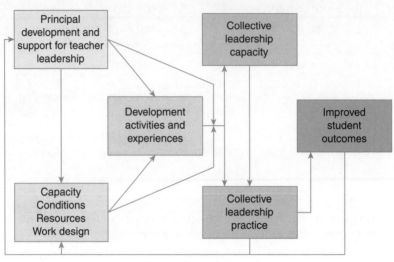

Collective Leadership Development

Administrative Support

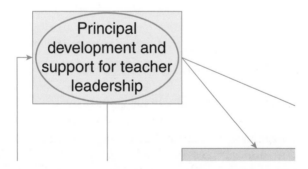

The principal helps set and sustain the vision and strategy
for collective leadership development. His or her support directly
influences four primary areas: teachers' capacity for leadership,

working conditions, resources, and work design. While these areas overlap, each presents interesting challenges and opportunities. We examine these four areas briefly (See Smylie & Eckert, 2017 for more detail on the model).

Collective leadership is not about the principals getting out of the way or using it as political cover for unpopular decisions.

- Ben is a high school math teacher. He believes that his department chair and principal are out to make his life miserable. Standards keep changing, common assessments are now mandated, and he loses much of his planning time to his professional learning community. If he could just get them off his back, close his door, and do what he loves— teaching math—his life would be so much better.

- Sarah is an outstanding third-year middle school teacher. By every metric—test scores, evaluations, peer/ student/parent opinion—she is one of the strongest teachers at her school. Any time her principal wants to do something new, she uses Sarah as an example of what quality teaching can look like and evidence of her outstanding leadership.

Collective leadership is working side by side and making the right decisions.

- Ali used to think that administrators getting out of the way best served teacher leadership. Then she went to Glenn O. Swing Elementary. This elementary school ranks in the 99th percentile of all elementary schools in the state, and 90.7% of students qualify for free and reduced lunch. She made several observations about the school that are pertinent to leadership development (Wright, 2016):

1. The principal sets the tone for the culture and intentionally builds leadership capacity.
2. The principal listens to teachers and creates roles based on student need and teacher expertise.

(Continued)

(Continued)

3. Everyone (including the principal) co-teaches.

4. There is an emphasis on student work.

5. The school schedule is built around teacher collaboration that is teacher led.

In your school, how does the principal develop teacher leadership? Is your experience more like Ben, Sarah, or Ali's?

Capacity

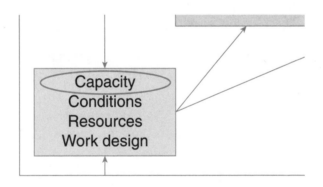

The capacity of the teachers for leadership work is central to the transformation of a school. Capacity can be constrained or supported by many factors, such as preparation (Darling-Hammond, Bransford, LePage, Hammerness, & Duffy, 2005; Jensen, Roberts-Hull, Magee, & Ginnivan, 2016), professional development (Darling-Hammond, Wei, Andree, Richardson, & Orphanos, 2009; Jensen, Sonnemann, Roberts-Hull, & Hunter, 2016), or colleagues (Hattie, 2015; Jackson & Bruegmann, 2009; Ronfeldt, Farmer, McQueen, & Grissom, 2015). If teachers are already at capacity with their instructional responsibilities, adding additional work—even if it is meaningful—will not necessarily improve outcomes for students (Eckert, Ulmer, Khatchatryan, & Ledesma, 2016). Teachers cannot do more than their capacity allows. Their initial capacity, as well as capacity that can be developed must be considered in this model. In practice, this means not allowing a beginning teacher to take on so many responsibilities beyond the classroom that this work becomes detrimental to instruction. On the other end of the spectrum, this means not expecting the twenty-five-year veteran teacher to just keep adding more leadership work without support.

Capacity is something that is malleable and can grow through deliberate practice. Deliberate practice is not just experience, it is practice that includes feedback, reflection, and opportunities for improvement (Ericsson, Krampe, & Tesch-Romer, 1993). In schools, we know that this occurs best with other educators. Over a ten-year period, teachers working in schools with strong professional environments improved 38 percent more than peers in schools with weak environments (Kraft & Papay, 2016).

Collective leadership is not about a formal title, "appoint and anoint," or "empower and flower."

Mark Smylie wrote eloquently about the problematic nature of "appoint and anoint" (Smylie & Denny, 1990), which he described as the teacher leadership development prevalent in the 1980s. A principal simply named a teacher to a new position—for example, department chair, grade-level leader, mentor—and miraculously leadership would occur.

On the other end of the spectrum, but actually a similar approach to development, is the trend that sees administrators seeking to empower teachers in the hopes that their leadership will miraculously flourish (Smylie & Eckert, 2017). Accordingly, just give teachers space, and leadership will bubble up. They are exhorted to "speak truth to power" and to "bust" through the organizational, administrative, and institutional "cages" that constrain them (Hess, 2015).

(Continued)

(Continued)

The commonality between these two approaches is that very little if any attention is paid to the development of leaders or followers. The first method can breed resentment when leadership feels like a club. The second can feel undirected and unaligned with school goals. Either approach makes leadership unsustainable and less impactful.

Collective leadership is formal and informal and the work determines the leader.

Collective leadership is determined by the leadership work dictated by the school's mission. Of course, this implies that teachers and administrators must be engaged in the development of the school's mission and subsequent adjustments to that mission. However, once the mission and goals are established through a school improvement plan or other mechanism, the work should identify the individuals who need development opportunities to do that work. The best way for the development to occur is for teachers and administrators to collaborate on designing, implementing, and tracking shared goals that will result in better outcomes for students.

Consider this example of leadership. He is a high school social studies teacher in a large urban district in Colorado. He began working with his current principal eight years ago and followed him to the school where they currently work. He has worked with his principal on behalf of their students for so long, that he can walk into his office and say, "Yo, you don't know what the hell you are doing." He has the autonomy to push back on ideas because he has the trust of his principal. Their work together serving marginalized student populations resulted in a half-time release position for him to support other teachers in the district.

What has been your experience with teacher leadership development? (Check all that apply.)

___ Appoint and anoint

___ Empower and flower

___ Leadership determined and developed by the work

Based on your experience, what are the implications of these approaches to development?

If you are a teacher, what is one thing you want your principal to know about your leadership capacity?

If you are an administrator, what is one thing you want teacher leaders to know about your approach to development of capacity?

Conditions

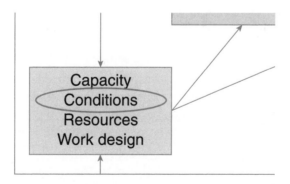

School conditions can break down into four areas of analysis: structure, culture, social conditions, and politics. We know that these conditions matter because teacher leadership is socially distributed and develops over time. Teachers need deliberate practice that allows them to reflect on what they are learning with others so that they become more comfortable dealing with failures, successes, and difficult situations (Szczesiul & Huizenga, 2015). What follows is a brief description of these conditions:

Structure is the way in which the school is organized: for example, departments, grade levels, teaching assignments, technology, administrative roles, support staff, physical arrangement, and time allocation.

- Culture is the way things are done in the school: for example, what is meaningful work, who really leads the school, how are students viewed, how involved are parents, and how engaged is the school with the community?
- Social conditions refer to the relationships among administrators: for example, administrators and teachers, teachers and other teachers, teachers and paraprofessionals, educators and students, students and other students, and educators and parents.
- Politics refers to the power dynamics that are in play in every school: for example, who are the movers and shakers who gets things done? who keeps things from getting done? do administrators support teachers? do teachers support administrators? and how does the school interface with the different contexts in which it is located—community, district, state, and national?

All of these conditions are important to consider because they can have a significant impact on a school's orientation and movement toward improvement.

Collective leadership is not always instructional, always saying "yes," or waiting for permission.

In the interviews I conducted with teachers and administrators, several recurring and problematic ideas surfaced. Teachers are interested in developing their leadership, but often they are working in conditions where it feels impossible. They are dealing with initiative-fatigue. One teacher described her context this way, "Decisions come from administration, and they are not always thought through. Communication is a problem. Then there is a new idea so they decide to blow the [old] idea up and do something different." However, in order to have influence, some teacher leaders feel they have to say "yes" to any new direction prescribed by a supervisor.

Conversely, they feel that they have to ask permission to step outside of their instructional role. Teachers feel marginalized when it comes to any decisions that extend beyond their own classrooms. The same teacher described what is needed in her district:

> There are teacher leaders in the district, despite the district. I don't want to come off like the district does not support us, but we have to have a lot of gumption to do it. Because we are a small school, if there is a project I want to do I have the ability to walk down the hall and make time for the project's key people.

Collective leadership is about equity and education policy, sometimes saying "no," and doing what needs to be done.

A nationally recognized teacher leader recently reminded me that "'No' is a complete sentence." Another teacher leader described her reason for leaving the school she had been at for the past three years and moving to a new one:

> I had such a hard time getting them to understand just how racist and systemic things were that I think it was part of their decision to help me find a better school. But I made an impact. There is now a fifteen-person school equity team, and they are calling and asking me for help. That is impact.

Bobbi Ciriza Houtchens is an amazing educator I highlighted in *The Novice Advantage*. I met her during our teacher leadership fellowship at the U.S. Department of Education. She was always quick to say "no" to anything that took her away from her focus on English learners and other marginalized student

(Continued)

(Continued)

populations. She also was the most gracious person I have ever met in not taking "no" for an answer. I followed her in to many meetings on and around Capitol Hill where she walked in and announced to the organizers, "We are teacher leaders from the U.S. Department of Education" and we walked right in. She then made use of every opportunity to advocate for students.

On a scale of 1 to 10, how willing are you take on leadership work?

1 = "I will lead only when my supervisor tells me to."

10 = "I am the Rosa Parks of leadership—I do whatever the work demands."

1   2   3   4   5   6   7   8   9   10

How have you seen teacher leaders step beyond instructional roles, say "no," or advocate for better educational policies?

Resources

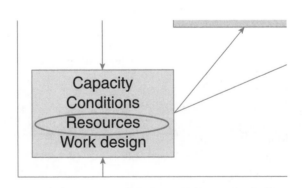

Primarily, "resources" for collective leadership development refers to time and money. Typically, time and money are synonymous as time for leadership development is contingent on the availability of money to cover the cost of that time. In many schools that I observed, there is a desire for teacher leadership development, but the lack of resources allocated to that end indicates different priorities. For example, in one urban district, teachers were expected to meet regularly with their PLCs, but no common time was built into the contractual workday. In schools like this, lack of resources, or at minimum competing resource allocation priorities, impede progress.

Work Design

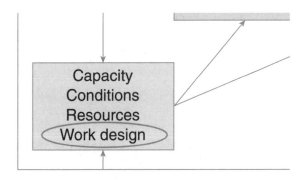

Building on the work of organizational science research (Hackman & Oldham, 1980), we need to consider how work is designed first as it relates to leadership development, and second how it relates to all the work that is done in schools. Schools have tinkered around the edges with PLC time, department chairs, grade-level teams, and myriad committees for school improvement. What does the work look like? How might schools consider redesigning the work of teachers and administrators to better support student outcomes?

Collective leadership is not task delegation, pseudo-administration, or more committee work.

Sometimes collective leadership is just delegation of work—mint officers, protocol keepers, note-takers, and so on. Sometimes collective leadership is seen as a means of "deepening the bench" of future administrators. Sometimes leadership is just another committee meeting.

One teacher in Florida described a district-wide leadership task force. "About 150 of us go to monthly meetings with the superintendent. He tells us what he is trying to accomplish, and how excited he is about the work. Then we are supposed to report back to our schools." When I asked if he ever sought the feedback of the teacher leaders, the answer was a definitive, "No." Not surprisingly, the superintendent resigned at the end of that school year.

Collective leadership is flexible, boundary spanning, meaningful work toward school goals.

Collective leadership can lead to administrative roles for teachers. Hopefully, a superintendent who had been a teacher leader previously would not make the mistakes described above. In fact, the good administrators I meet are the ones who still miss the classroom and see their roles as extending their influence to impact and support the work they loved doing in the classroom. The best ones go back and co-teach or teach at any opportunity. However, teacher leadership must be flexible, and find its meaning in the improvement of outcomes for students. This flexibility must serve the boundary spanning that teacher leadership requires—bridging, buffering, syncing, and transforming (Aldrich & Herker, 1977; Ernst & Chroot-Mason, 2010; Goldring, 1997).

Teacher leaders and students at a rural high school developed a program for sophomore students who are in honors English and math. Four teachers collaborated with students to develop classes where, over the course of two years, students can work on projects of their own choosing that meet Common Core State Standards for math and English Language Arts. In the first semester of their sophomore years, for 135 minutes a day, students receive instruction in both subjects. The second semester, they work on a project that they identified has a community emphasis. These projects ranged from blacksmithing manuals to leadership development. One of the students, who did not know how to code before the project, because of this work, earned an internship as a website analyst.

How does your school approach leadership?

At your school, is leadership development prescriptive or flexible?

On a scale of 1 to 10, how does your school develop teacher leaders?

1 = "Teacher leaders are future principals who love paperwork and bureaucracy."

10 = "We are the school equivalent of Google—we innovate constantly based on the needs of our students and skills of our leaders."

1	2	3	4	5	6	7	8	9	10

Development Activities and Experiences

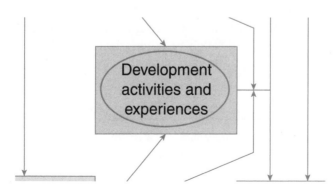

School leadership development activities and experiences are dependent on principal support, teacher capacity, and school conditions, and reflect the strengths and weaknesses of the factors that influence them. Meaningful leadership development activities and experiences are about the work required to move the school forward toward meeting its goals.

Perhaps the best way to understand this is to understand what is not school leadership development and why educators view so many activities and experiences cynically. A teacher might describe the experience this way:

> Over the summer, a principal will read a book, part of a book, maybe even just the introduction to a book—highlight a few things and then that is what our development is supposed to revolve around for the year. I understand. Principals are super busy and looking for anything to help. The highlighted idea might be something like formative assessment, standards-based grading, or Japanese lesson study. The principal starts off really excited about the idea in August, then reality hits and everything is forgotten by September.

This is directly related to the design of the leadership work. If the design fails to account for all the elements that must influence the work done in the activities and experience, it will be forgotten. Contrast this teacher's description with what occurs at the rural high school (described above) where administrators, teachers, and students go on a two-day retreat in each spring to design the school improvement plan that will drive the mission for the following year. That retreat will be a much more impactful experience than a team-building exercise, which is the difference between doing actual leadership work and trite team-building exercises. I doubt schools have improved much by having teachers fall blindly into the arms of colleagues—leadership development via trust falls.

Increased Capacity and Improved Practice

If the leadership experiences are effective, then leadership capacity increases and leadership practice improves. However, the principal's support, teacher leaders' initial capacity, and school

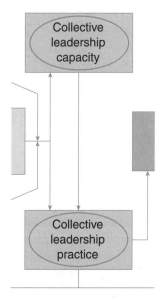

conditions can catalyze or limit the impact of the leadership work even after the development activities. For example, a principal sends a fourth-year teacher to Columbia University for a summer institute on how to build grade-level teams. She comes back excited to share what she has learned with her third-grade team. The institute gave her all types of strategies for how to engage colleagues.

The bad news: no one is interested in working with her.

Why not?

There could be many reasons, but if nothing was done to prepare the teachers who did not go to the institute to follow, then that was an oversight. If the teachers who were left behind were veteran teachers who resented a relative novice going in their place, then the social and political dynamics of the team were ignored. If no time was provided to work together when the teacher returned, then structures and resources were ignored. All of these issues confound leadership development in many schools.

Contrast this with the suburban high school time I observed and its PLC time. I was at their bi-weekly meeting where school begins an hour late so that teachers can collaborate. In an English PLC, eight teachers were meeting, all with student work samples on their Chromebooks. The PLC leader took notes on a shared Google doc agenda. The PLC leader said to one of the newer teachers on the team, "Do you want to tell us about the standards-based grading conference?"

The teacher immediately began sharing about a Rick Wormeli conference that she and a number of other teachers from the school had attended. "He talked a lot about formative and summative assessments and how students should be able to take assessments until they had the score they wanted. On rubrics, we should only show students what is excellent on a rubric because that is what they should be striving for."

Several of the veteran teachers pushed back. "How would this work logistically?" "I think these immediate retakes are ridiculous. If it is multiple choice, you just pick another option."

Another teacher replied, "I think it is about our feedback, not the assessment. There needs to be a more specific link between our feedback and the assessment. We can't keep writing things like 'needs more development' without giving direction for how to do this."

I was able to observe a chemistry PLC on a late-start day and saw the way decisions on curriculum and assessment were made. There were five chemistry, and one special education teacher meeting together. They were working on a lab that required a fairly complex procedure, volumetric dilution. Only one of the teachers had done this before, a first-year teacher who had previously been a bench chemist. He took the lead as they worked through the lab procedures. While they were working on the lab, the special education teacher was pulling up names and scores on the computer to identify students who needed support in each of the chemistry sections. As two of the teachers were working specifically on the dilution, the other three were discussing when the lab should be done and how to better manage the Chromebooks. After they completed the lab preparation, all six teachers began revision of a common assessment by discussing prior student performance. The work, not roles or personalities or top-down administration, was driving and contributing to their development as leaders.

The work, not roles or personalities or top-down administration, was driving and contributing to their development as leaders.

Collective leadership is not about teacher "buy-in" or fearful accountability.

I cringe every time I hear an administrator talk about getting teacher "buy-in." Many are well meaning and just using a term that they believe is innocuous, and it may be. However, sometimes "buy-in" means that a decision has been made, that decision is being "sold," and teachers need to get on board. Typically, this occurs in top-down mandates that are born out of fear. For example, superintendents are concerned about test scores, so they begin to push for common assessments in every subject. In fact, the assessments are given on the same days in every class in their districts. This is the kind of idea where superintendents are looking for "buy-in."

Collective leadership is sharing ownership, expertise, and fearless improvement.

What the superintendents should have been looking for is shared expertise. If they are concerned about student outcomes, why wouldn't they enlist the expertise of the teachers who are entrusted with their education? Maybe they arrive at common assessments, but the solution has a much higher probability of success with a consultative if not collaborative approach (Hackman & Oldham, 1980).

I am currently facilitating the work of a 13,000-student district that is moving away from salary steps for experience in their collectively bargained teacher contract. We have two years to develop a recommendation for the teacher's union and school board. The team consists of nine administrators and nine teachers. Changing how people are compensated is hard work, but through the process of studying and collective evidence of possible options we are developing expertise that would not have been possible without the collaboration. I do not know what the recommendation will be, but our goal is improvement, not perfection. And certainly not buy-in.

Does your school operate out of fearful accountability or fearless improvement?

(Continued)

(Continued)

One a scale of 1 to 10, where does your school fall?

1 = "They (evil externality) make us do everything."

10 = "We may fail, but we fail forward."

| 1 | 2 | 3 | 4 | 5 | 6 | 7 | 8 | 9 | 10 |

Do administrators in your district want teacher buy in or teacher expertise?

One a scale of 1 to 10, where does your principal fall?

1 = "Buy-in. This is good for you…. because I say it is."

10 = "Expertise. I don't decide anything without teacher expertise."

| 1 | 2 | 3 | 4 | 5 | 6 | 7 | 8 | 9 | 10 |

Student Outcomes

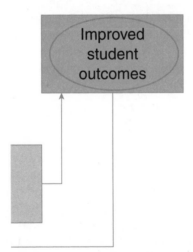

While it is too early to tell what the impact of this type of leadership development on student outcomes will be, the work that these educators are doing, with the support of their principal, is transforming them as leaders. The work dictates who will lead, not seniority, personality type, or position, nor an administrator who "appoints and anoints" (Smylie & Denny, 1990). Because the work is done by teachers who are at the technical core of the educational enterprise, it seems plausible that this will impact teaching practice, which in turn impacts student outcomes.

In fact, this is already occurring. In 2013, Iowa launched a Teacher Leadership and Compensation System (TLC). The goal of TLC is to improve educational opportunity for all Iowa public school students by creating a classroom-based leadership corps in each district prepared to support students and colleagues adaptively. The state hopes this approach will attract and retain effective teachers, promote collaboration, reward professional growth and effective teaching, and ultimately improve student achievement. Iowa has invested heavily in this, allocating $50 million per year to support districts' design and implementation of TLC models that respond to local student and educator needs.

For the past three years, we have been tracking one Iowa district's implementation of the TLC. Teachers and administrators report statistically significant increases in their ability to work well together in order to improve student outcomes (see sidebar).

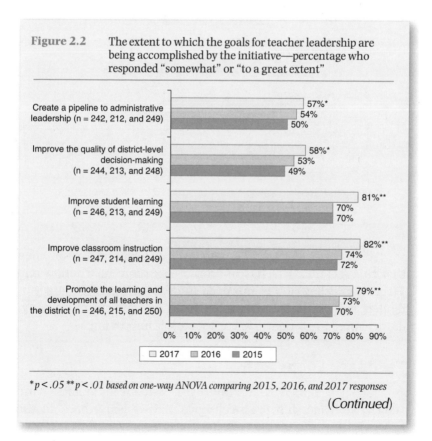

Figure 2.2   The extent to which the goals for teacher leadership are being accomplished by the initiative—percentage who responded "somewhat" or "to a great extent"

*p < .05 **p < .01 based on one-way ANOVA comparing 2015, 2016, and 2017 responses

(Continued)

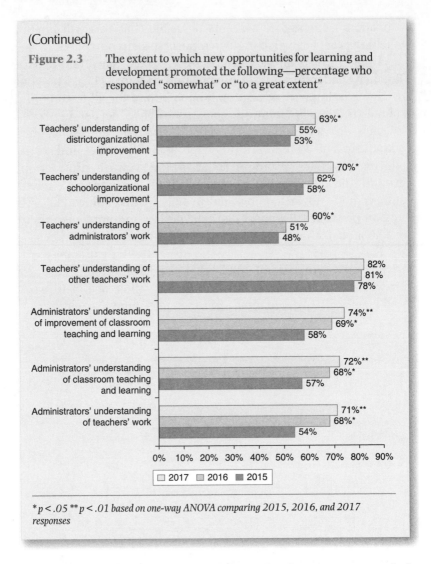

(Continued)

Figure 2.3   The extent to which new opportunities for learning and development promoted the following—percentage who responded "somewhat" or "to a great extent"

Teachers' understanding of districtorganizational improvement: 63%* / 55% / 53%

Teachers' understanding of schoolorganizational improvement: 70%* / 62% / 58%

Teachers' understanding of administrators' work: 60%* / 51% / 48%

Teachers' understanding of other teachers' work: 82% / 81% / 78%

Administrators' understanding of improvement of classroom teaching and learning: 74%** / 69%* / 58%

Administrators' understanding of classroom teaching and learning: 72%** / 68%* / 57%

Administrators' understanding of teachers' work: 71%** / 68%* / 54%

□ 2017   ▨ 2016   ■ 2015

*$p < .05$ **$p < .01$ based on one-way ANOVA comparing 2015, 2016, and 2017 responses

Across the district, 74 percent of educators responded that the TLC initiative has improved classroom instruction and 70 percent believe it has improved student learning. The superintendent reports that teacher retention is up and student learning, as measured by standardized test scores, is improving.

Feedback Loops

You will notice that "improved student outcomes" and "collective leadership practice" have arrows going back to the

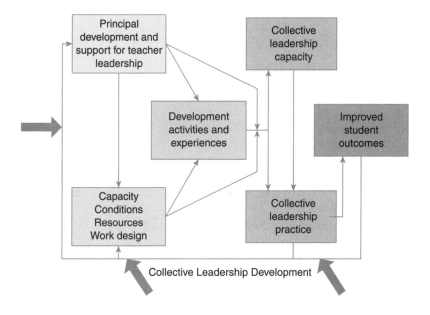

antecedent factors that influence development: principal development, capacity, conditions, resources, and work design. As teacher leadership practice and student outcomes improve, they must inform these areas. The development of leadership necessarily influences the organizational conditions in which it is developed. For this reason, the model is about more than teacher leadership development. The model really represents school improvement through collective leadership development of both teachers and administrators.

LEADERSHIP DEVELOPMENT READINESS

Now we need to apply the model as a lens. How ready is your school to develop collective leadership? To answer that question, use a diagnostic tool that is a compromise between brevity and nuance. With only fifteen probes, it may not be able to definitely determine everything important about your school. However, this is a significantly more realistic tool than a survey of over 300 probes that takes thirty to forty-five minutes to complete like the survey I shared from Iowa. At the very least, this diagnostic tool is a good place to start conversations at your school about next steps to developing leadership that meets the needs of your context.

2.2 WHAT CAN WE DO RIGHT NOW?

Complete the following Leadership Development Readiness (LDR) tool to rate YOUR SCHOOL. Teachers should use the first response column and administrators use the second.

Leadership Development Readiness (LDR) Tool: 1 = strongly disagree, 5 = strongly agree

Probe	Teacher	Administrator
1. There is a shared vision of what collective (administrators and teachers together) leadership should look like at our school.	1 2 3 4 5	1 2 3 4 5
2. The principal is comfortable expanding the power of teachers.	1 2 3 4 5	1 2 3 4 5
3. There are teachers who have the ability to work with and help other teachers improve their practice.	1 2 3 4 5	1 2 3 4 5
4. There are teachers who can think through problems well and come up with innovative solutions.	1 2 3 4 5	1 2 3 4 5
5. There is a high degree of relational trust at our school.	1 2 3 4 5	1 2 3 4 5
6. There is sufficient time for teachers and administrators to develop leadership.	1 2 3 4 5	1 2 3 4 5
7. There are sufficient financial resources for teachers and administrators to develop leadership.	1 2 3 4 5	1 2 3 4 5
8. Administrators and teachers work well together.	1 2 3 4 5	1 2 3 4 5
9. Communication flows effectively from administrators to teachers.	1 2 3 4 5	1 2 3 4 5

Probe	Teacher	Administrator
10. Communication flows effectively from teachers to administrators.	1 2 3 4 5	1 2 3 4 5
11. Our school is a safe place to take risks.	1 2 3 4 5	1 2 3 4 5
12. Teachers at our school are solutions-oriented.	1 2 3 4 5	1 2 3 4 5
13. Administrators at our school are solutions-oriented.	1 2 3 4 5	1 2 3 4 5
14. My work is structured in such a way that I can improve with others.	1 2 3 4 5	1 2 3 4 5
15. Collective leadership development will improve student outcomes.	1 2 3 4 5	1 2 3 4 5
Total:	_____ /75	_____ /75
Average of all responses (teachers and administrators):	_____ /75	
Difference between teacher and administrator averages:	_____	

After you complete the diagnostic tool, total the score in your column. Hopefully, you are doing this with other teachers and administrators. If so, average the scores of all of the respondents and record. Here are some guidelines for how to interpret that score:

Average Score	Interpretation
60–75	Clearly some leadership development has already occurred and your school is ready for more.
45–59	Your school has some elements in place to develop collective leadership, but some further discussion is needed.

(Continued)

(Continued)

Average Score	Interpretation
30–44	Proceed cautiously. Look carefully at the items and determine where there are areas that need particular attention before moving ahead.
15–29	The elements that are required to move ahead effectively are not present. Look for areas of particular weakness and begin conversations there.

The other score that really matters is the difference between the teacher average and the administrator average (for simplicity, record the difference as a positive number). If there is a disparity between averages, this could be evidence of a need for development in particular areas. Typically, administrators rate these items more positively than teachers, so this can lead to honest conversations about differences in perceptions. Below are some guidelines to help with interpretation:

Difference between averages	Interpretation
0–5	Teachers and administrators are on the same page. They perceive opportunities and challenges related to leadership development in similar ways.
6–15	Teachers and administrators are pretty well aligned in their perceptions. Determine where there are discrepancies and discuss before moving ahead.
16–30	Proceed cautiously. There are significant differences in perceptions. Collaborative, transparent conversations are needed.
31+	Before doing anything else, spend time discussing how this difference is possible. A third party might be necessary to help administrators and teachers hear each other's perspectives.

THE FOUR RS APPLIED TO SCHOOLS

After two decades in education, I know that all I can do is offer you evidence and ideas that you can adapt and apply to your own specific context. Hopefully you know a bit more about your context after using the LDR. Every student is different and therefore every school is different. In *The Novice Advantage: Fearless Practice for Every Teacher*, I introduced the Four Rs as a way to approach the ideas in the book. Most of us do this anyway when we are exposed to new ideas, but I want to emphasize the need to practice this approach.

Building on the concepts behind Networked Improvement Communities (Bryk, Gomez, Grunow, & LeMahieu, 2015), this model can be adapted for school improvement as well. Schools, and leadership teams in particular, need school learning networks (SLNs) that inform what they do (See Figure 2.1).

Schools are always looking to improve, and their SLNs should inform those efforts. Typically, good administrators have these kinds of networks as they think about school and district improvement. However, involving teacher leaders in these

Figure 2.4   The 4 Rs for Schools

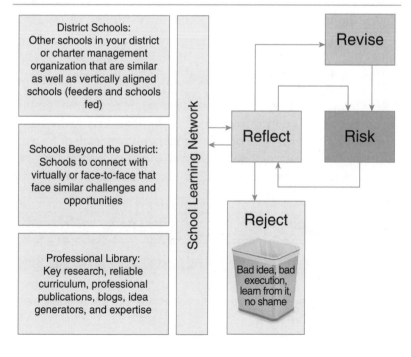

types of connections can be vital for gaining new insights into challenges, particularly instructional issues. These SLNs are composed of schools in the district or charter management organization that are similar, or feed, or are fed by a particular school. I am always amazed when I study a district to see how many schools are dealing with the same issues, but believe they are dealing with challenges that are unique to them because they have not had the opportunity to engage other leaders in their own districts. The SLNs should also include schools beyond these immediate connections. These connections can be virtual or face-to-face, but they are invaluable for seeing challenges from different perspectives. The last piece of the SLN is the professional library—the key research, reliable curriculum, publications, blogs, idea generators, and expertise that can inform the leadership work.

After reflection, the school leadership team has to take a risk. This cannot be haphazard risk-taking. Schools are filled with students who become the collateral damage of failed experiments. That is why we inform our risks with our SLNs.

After taking the risk, the school must collect evidence of the impact of the risk, unblinkingly and honestly. After the evidence is collected, the school must decide whether to continue with the initiative, revise, or reject. There is no shame in rejecting a bad idea—sometimes an idea just does not work in a given context. The only shame is continuing a bad idea because you aren't even collecting evidence of its negative impact.

Sometimes evidence will end an initiative, and occasionally it will catalyze another. So often initiatives start with great fanfare and expectation and are scrapped before they even really had a chance to succeed. The Four Rs process allows leaders to truly evaluate the impact of new initiatives. After collecting that evidence, as responsible members of SLNs, schools must share their

2.3 WHAT CAN WE DO RIGHT NOW?

On a scale of 1 to 10, how good is your school at using the Four Rs to evaluate risks?

1 = "We change initiatives weekly based on the gut feelings of our superintendent."

10 = "We constantly reflect and course correct based on evidence."

1   2   3   4   5   6   7   8   9   10

What is your school or district doing now that is working well for teachers and students?

How do you know?

What other schools or districts are part of your school's learning network?

What other resources do you need to add to your school's learning network?

success and course corrections so that all schools in the network can learn and grow with them.

THE IDEAL SCHOOL REVISITED

I cannot yet envision what the ideal school looks like. I would probably fail this design challenge. The good thing is that *I* do not have to design the school. In fact, *I* should not be designing schools. What I have tried to do in this chapter is describe a model that allows local educators the opportunity to *create and sustain* an ideal school over time.

Together, teachers, administrators, and students are already creating these schools. If we understand that different contexts require different solutions and that the only certainty is change, then we know all we can do is to create conditions and opportunities for leadership to flourish. That leadership must be built on student outcomes that are agreed on by a school community. I cannot offer a prescription for how to do this, but I was able to use this model as a lens to collect evidence of the kind of leadership development that is transforming schools. Consider the schools mentioned in Chapters 3 through 5 as part of your SLN. After reflection, what risks will you take and what will you reject or revise?

2.4 WHAT CAN WE DO RIGHT NOW?

Start developing the Collective Leadership Map. Spend some time thinking about an adaptive challenge that your school faces. This has to be something that is significant—something that requires a shift in mindset. Just try to identify the challenge and begin thinking about the people in the building who could develop a collective leadership solution. We re-visit this map in Chapter 7.

Figure 2.5   Collective Leadership Map

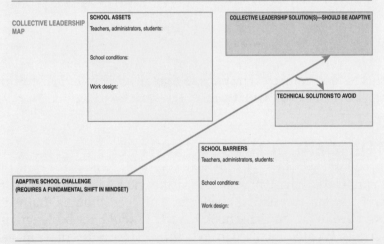

NOTE: A full-scale version of the Collective Leadership Map is available for your use on page 196.

Chapter Review: What Matters Most for Schools (and in This Chapter)?

❖ Teacher leadership is not a panacea.

❖ Collective leadership needs to be part of an adaptive solution to adaptive challenges.

❖ We cannot design theoretical ideal schools. We need to develop systems of leadership development that can adapt to complex contexts.

❖ Leadership development for school improvement must include teachers and principals. Capacity, conditions, resources, and work design influence development in meaningful ways.

❖ Collective leadership practice and student outcomes must impact development.

❖ School learning networks are essential for informing risk taking.

❖ Schools must collect evidence of impact and share that evidence with others.

Action Steps

1. After using the Leadership Development Readiness (LDR) tool and the Collective Leadership Map, what have you realized about your school? What surprised you? What didn't surprise you?

2. What do you think about Probes 9 and 10 as well as 12 and 13? Are there differences between these items? What do your answers tell you about your school?

3. Is there anything that you think is missing in the Collective Leadership Development Model?

4. Talk to each other about the results of the LDR tool. Be as transparent as you can be about the results.

5. What excites you about the results?

6. What concerns you about the results?

7. *For administrators:* What do you really want teachers to know about leadership development at your school?

8. *For teachers:* What do you really want your administrator(s) to know about leadership development at your school?

CHAPTER 3

The Rural Grassroots

"You have to study this school."

If you are thinking that the rural high school's profile on the following page does not seem that remarkable, that is what I thought as well. This school appears to be like many of the thousands of rural schools across the country—dwindling student population, some poverty, and many students not ready for college. However, when I described my research on leadership development, the Illinois State Superintendent of Schools told me, "You have to study this school."

How did he find this school in the middle of the cornfields of Illinois? He met a National Board Certified math teacher at an awards dinner. In a brief conversation, she told him about some of the things happening at her high school. She "did not think much more about it" until a few weeks later when he showed up at her school to see what they were doing.

Eventually, the numbers in the school profile might reflect the work that is already occurring at this school; however, what is so interesting about this school are some of the leading indicators that communicate so much more than these numbers. Like the state superintendent, I made a call to the principal and set up a visit to the school. And I kept coming back.

Due to an economic downturn, businesses were leaving the community served by this school district. Over the past eight years, the school lost over 150 students, requiring the principal,

The Rural High School Profile (Numbers are approximate to maintain anonymity):

 Total Enrollment: <500

 Instructional Spending Per Pupil: approximately $6,000

 Low-Income Students: >35%

 English Learners: <5%

 Students with Disabilities: >10%

 Graduation Rate: >85%

 Ready for College: >40%

5Essentials School Environment:

> Effective Leaders: Average Implementation
>
> Collaborative Teachers: Average Implementation

through a reduction in force, to release seven teachers. Those seven teachers represent over 20 percent of the teaching force. Under these circumstances, some schools and school leaders would move into a defensive posture to try to protect whatever resources and interests remained. That was not this school's story. Before you read more about this school, take a few minutes to work through Part II of the Collective Leadership Inventory.

ADMINISTRATIVE SUPPORT

The high school was built in the 1930s as part of Franklin Roosevelt's Works Progress Administration. The school has had

Collective Leadership Inventory	
What leadership development efforts receive the most resources at your school?	
What leadership development efforts need additional resources? Rank your top three choices.	
How are students engaged in leadership development efforts?	
Without any additional resources, how could you develop collective leadership among students, teachers, and administrators?	
Rate the following: Improved leadership development at this school can only happen with additional resources.	Strongly Disagree Strongly Agree 1 2 3 4 5 6 7 8 9 10

multiple additions over the ensuing eighty years, but the original structure still remains—including an impressive marble entryway. Before entering the building however, there are a couple of permanent trailers located in the parking lot. This is the home of the district's central administration and its superintendent.

The superintendent's office looks more like that of a contractor running a construction site than the office of someone charged with running a school district. The office in a trailer was a fitting metaphor for the administration's fiscal priorities. In an environment where resources are scarce, any available money is plowed into the schools (elementary, middle, and high), and specifically, the classrooms. The office also fit the personality of the superintendent. He was a former high school math teacher, and his heart was still in the classroom, which is where the district's money appeared to be as well.

At the beginning of the school year, the superintendent shared with the teachers his desire for them to take risks. He acknowledged that failure is implicit in risk taking. This exhortation to take risks did not appear to be simple lip service or limited just to teachers. In many of the classrooms I entered, there were large posters on the walls with four words: "Experiment, Fail, Learn, Repeat."

The principal at this high school identified himself as an "accidental principal" who had taught for nineteen years and now believed in the philosophy of "leadership by laziness." His self-described philosophy was to hire good people and then let them lead.

> When they come to me, I do my absolute level best to say yes and find resources for them to do the work that needs to be done. We do our best to be innovative. Failures are OK—as long as they are not unethical—because we should take chances. Coherence [of leadership vision and strategy] is only compromised by hope. Even when I am 95 percent sure that something will not work, I will still let teachers move ahead with it.

This lack of coherence was problematic in this context as resources were scarce and sometimes teachers felt that the support they received was limited to verbal encouragement and little else. However, attempts were underway to increase coherence while continuing to allow for organic leadership opportunities. This is particularly challenging to do with shrinking resources. The primary shift that was occurring at the school was the development of a shared vision of leadership and what the school could become.

The school was developing an integrated School Improvement Plan (SIP) that involved administrators, teachers, and students. Written at a retreat in the spring, the SIP for the following year was a collaborative effort of administrators, teachers, and two student representatives. The team got away from the school for a couple of days and developed goals around identified needs. They examined work that was already occurring, work that should be expanded, and ideas that had not yet been tried. To do this analysis, they used the data that they generated from previous plans. Administrators, teachers, and students all brought their own expertise and perspectives to conversations, but the leadership work—not position, seniority, or politics—drove the plan to improve the school.

In interviews and focus groups, teachers repeatedly reported that their leadership work "bubbled up" from the needs that they and their students identified. One teacher described the

To better understand the holistic, shared, SMART (specific, measurable, attainable, realistic, timely) focus of the SIP goals, it is helpful to see some of their current goals:

1. One hundred percent of students will complete at least twenty community service hours per year. (The previous year, 42.5% of students completed twenty hours of community service.)

2. Increase by 5% per year the number of graduating seniors who participated in eight extracurricular activities in their high school career. (The previous year, 41% of graduates participated in eight extracurricular activities.)

   a. All teachers will use priority standard-aligned assessment data from a Rigorous Curriculum Design (RCD) unit they created to do the following: (The previous year, all departments created two RCD units.) Determine how much students learned based on both instruction and assessment results tied to the unit.

   b. Establish baseline data with a long-term goal of creating benchmarks aligned to priority standards to measure mastery for all courses.

   c. Teachers will provide an informal synopsis of their analysis by the start of second semester.

3. One hundred percent of students will be on track for graduation at the end of their sophomore, junior, and senior years. (The previous year, 90% of sophomores, 80% of juniors, and 89% of seniors were on track.)

leadership work that led to development this way: "As teacher leaders, we figure out ideas and then go get the blessing [from administrators] and just do it." Teacher leaders reiterated the need for contextualized leadership and administrative support. One teacher leader said,

> We are really supported by the administration. I think that is critical because of our small size, things from cities or suburbs are not necessarily going to work with our population. Or, just with the fact that we have all these single-tons [one teacher per subject], a lot of our things that I would call successes have come from the fact that we are supported by our administration for our own ideas.

CAPACITY

This level of trust was predicated on the administrators' belief that teachers and students have a high degree of capacity to lead. There is good reason for this trust.

3.1 WHAT CAN WE DO RIGHT NOW?

On a scale of 1 to 10, how well does your school balance support for grassroots ideas with coherence?

1 = "Coherence is easy. We do exactly what the principal wants."

10 = "Every idea gets traction, but we have no idea how anything fits together."

1   2   3   4   5   6   7   8   9   10

Does your school need more ideas or more coherence? Both?

Depending on the answer to the last question, what steps do teachers and administrators need to take to make that happen?

The principal proudly shared,

> I have two teachers who were finalists for Illinois Teacher of the Year, and six National Board Certified Teachers (NBCTs). This is a building of people who build positive relationships with kids. Most of the things we are looking for are teacher led. Teachers write the SIP. We are trying to get kids involved. They are going to meet off-site to bring in social emotional learning and academic goals.

In this small high school, there are six NBCTs and two finalists for Illinois Teacher of the Year. That means almost a quarter of the full-time teachers are NBCTs. The principal, assistant principal, and department chairs all cited "having the right people on the bus" (Collins, 2001) and encouraging them to grow together. An upper division math NBCT was the primary catalyst and supporter of other teachers in the district going through the National Board process. She became the National Board coordinator for the district and supports elementary, middle, and high school teachers in the district. The ability of this teacher to support other teachers helped build capacity throughout the system. Other teachers cited her support in the National Board process as being "invaluable," and also described their work together as "building community."

She described the types of people who do the leadership work at her school. "Those people are really positive. They are really upbeat. And they don't have to have the credit, they just want to see the work get done and get done well." This is a recurring theme across schools and interviews: Educators with the greatest capacity for leadership view leadership as being about the work, not the person.

> *Educators with the greatest capacity for leadership view leadership as being about the work, not the person.*

Every educator in the high school was seen as a potential leader. Several years ago, a paraprofessional noted that many of the students in the school community had not been more than thirty miles away from their town, and almost 25 percent of the high school students were not participating in any extracurricular activities. To address this issue, she approached the principal with the idea of "Club 9." Club 9 stands for seven people, a driver, and an idea. Students propose a location, get six other students to agree, a driver, a school van, and they go. "At first, I just asked for gas money. Now we have the trips cleared by the district lawyer. Kids that were not involved in school are more engaged." Students are planning trips to major cities from Memphis to Boston, to places ranging from symphony halls to art museums to aquariums, and to activities from scuba diving to ice skating.

The Origin of Club 9 According to the Founder

"I do not need the credit for everything I do. And that is the beautiful thing. You can throw an idea out there. On the School Improvement Committee in 2012 and 2013, we were talking about getting kids more involved in school. We were up to 22 to 24% of kids who don't do anything. We talked about this in our [homeroom] meetings, what else can we do with this twenty minutes a day? Maybe some enrichment-type things? And it was going back and forth. Then one day some boy came up to me who was a junior, and I had the question of the day, 'Where have you been?' and he was like, 'Can I just have some candy?' And I am like, 'Well, where have you been?' He says, 'I have never been farther than [a town forty minutes away].' He was 17 years old and had never been out of the area. I called our superintendent, and I said, 'We want a van and we want to take some kids.' He said, 'write it up,' and we did. And that's kind of how it started. He said, 'I love that idea.' We didn't ask for anything more than some gas. I didn't ask to go too far to begin with. And then all of a sudden, people are throwing me money for this program and saying, 'can you go here, and there?'

But then, every time we wanted to go somewhere I needed board approval and eventually [the principal] said, 'This is ridiculous. We will just do it in-house as long as it will fly with the lawyers.' So eventually I get a note from the lawyers that said what we could do. So, I was like, 'OK. This gives me a lot of options.' I have some wonderful staff members who, um, there is one who gives me money regularly. She said, 'I did this with all my kids and I know it was important to

them and I want these kids to have a good time.' I had someone give me $20 because they didn't think one of the kids
could afford lunch when we went downtown. When I took
kids to Memphis, we got to see five states in three days with
that boy who said he had never been anywhere."

The principal described why this paraprofessional is a leader.
"I would say with our most marginalized kids, she is a leader. She
sees the struggles that these kids deal with every single day. She
knows who has been kicked out of their house and is bouncing
from a friend's couch to another friend's couch." Her relationships
with students are what make the leadership work successful.

This was a student-inspired idea, championed by a paraprofessional, and supported by administration. However, teachers
believe there is still more capacity in the building. One biology
teacher shared a common refrain, "There is still more capacity.
The people that are tapped all the time—that can be exhausting.
They feel the pressure of living up to that." In addition to the
strain placed on leaders in a small school, she described the potential personal cost: "As a leader, you have to put yourself out there.
It [your idea] might be shot down and you might look like an
idiot. I had this idea for a while, but was not comfortable enough
to bring it to our last principal."

Particularly in a context that depends on grassroots leadership, courage to advocate for needed work is a significant portion
of capacity. Building a culture with a shared vision for leadership
development is necessary. If ideas are not welcomed, capacity is
not expanded or capitalized on, and innovation is nearly impossible. Almost out of necessity, this
school was built on organic leadership that arose from identified needs.
Club 9 is a perfect example. Students
lacked cultural capital, but they had
an idea to expand their capital, a
paraprofessional advocated for them
to administration, and a new program
to broaden their cultural experiences
began.

Students lacked cultural capital, but they had an idea to expand their capital, a paraprofessional advocated for them to administration, and a new program to broaden their cultural experiences began.

> ### 3.2 WHAT CAN WE DO RIGHT NOW?
>
> What programs at your school need additional support?
>
> Most of us are passionate about programs that we start. How passionate are you about supporting others' ideas? What programs that others have developed need your support?

CONDITIONS AND RESOURCES

"At our size, if you do the work, you are the leader." This summed up the opportunities and challenges of small, rural school leadership. The teacher who shared this comment noted the exciting, yet daunting nature of this type of context. School conditions and resources impact any type of leadership work or development. At a school with a dwindling student population, commensurately shrinking budget, and repeated reductions in force, this is a pressing reality. Some teachers are the only teachers of their subject in the entire school. How can they collaborate?

If teachers have an idea, where do they find the resources?

This rural high school generated some creative solutions to challenging realities because administrators did whatever they could to say, "Yes." Whenever possible, administrative support was combined with additional resources. When asked if she is given any additional resources, the National Board coordinator said, "We can ask for them. I mean I asked for time the other day to go over to the elementary. During final review time when the portfolios are getting ready to be sent, I have said, 'Hey, can I go over and sit with these two teachers during this section of the day?'"

What was the administrative response? She said, "They have gotten me internal subs so I can do that. They can give me time if I ask for it."

The downside? "I just have to miss class time." Pitting leadership development against the immediate needs of students is a problem. This is the result of work structures and resources that do not match the aspirations of leadership.

This results in a perceived lack of time. Teachers reported rarely getting to see each other teach because those observations come at the cost of instructional time. This comment from a teacher is somewhat representative: "They are trying to get us together for collaboration, especially on the SIP, by giving us some subs. Personally, I don't like that because my main job here is to teach and I don't think I should be pulled out of my classroom." In order to find the time to meet, some teachers are getting together on Sunday afternoon to plan for cross-curricular work. This certainly is not ideal, nor should it be the model for finding time for leadership development. Some teachers in the school cannot meet outside of the school day. "There are some teachers who are leaders who like to have that time during their contract hours." This can lead to a lack of team and school cohesion.

3.3 WHAT CAN WE DO RIGHT NOW?

Which resources and conditions do you most depend on to improve your work?

What changes in resources and conditions have to happen for you to have more time to observe other teachers and have them observe you?

What are the next steps for accessing those resources and conditions?

WORK DESIGN

Unique challenges for work design exist for small schools. One teacher expressed her frustration as a whimsical aspiration:

> We don't know how to make things work within the framework [current work structure] that we have. A lot of us just say if we can just shut school down for a year and revamp the whole thing it would be amazing because there are so many incredible ideas out there. But we make it work as much as we can with the constraints that we have.

To illustrate, most teachers are not part of a formal PLC. There is one physical science teacher and two teachers of foreign language. Common planning time is difficult to find for people with even similar jobs. When collaborative work occurs, administrators cover classes or get sub coverage.

Attempts have been made to formally develop leadership. Several area districts have combined resources to send teachers through a leadership academy that was established by the district superintendent. Most leaders who participated speak highly of the academy, but the participation requires more time out of the classroom.

When time was made for teachers to collaborate, it was not always well received. Over the past several years, an attempt was made to develop leadership through data teams. An outside vendor provided training on use of student data to improve instruction. The results were disappointing. Below is a representative sentiment from both teachers and administrators:

> I thought it (data team) was a very good thing at first. I was all about creating our units, working through that process because I thought it was something that was really important and was going to help me reach students better. I think from there it became more about the format in which we were creating units than about the units themselves. And I think now because of that, there is a lot of pushback going on. We are finding for the science department that we are starting this process over from the beginning, which is painful. The data teams we set up here

are not very useful. I think the opportunity to create your own data teams is what we needed to begin with and we were not given that opportunity.

While not everyone is able to participate, the school has identified two key areas where collaboration among teams of four to five teachers is essential. To meet the needs of students, work for teachers has been re-designed by students and teachers.

Freshmen Team

In 2009, after analyzing data that some showed freshmen were not transitioning well to high school, teachers and administrators set aside common planning time to establish a "freshmen team" to better support them. They have one common planning period per day, and the team consists of a special educator, math teacher, history teacher, science teacher, counselor, paraprofessional, and assistant principal. In one meeting I observed, nine students were discussed with pertinent input from each member of the team. While typical in many middle schools, this type of structure is more unusual at high school. What was striking was the level of detail that each teacher was able to add to the composite picture of each student. For example, one student would not dress for PE. One of the teachers shared, "Her family is getting evicted. I am not sure she has anywhere to do laundry." Another added, "She won't wear shorts, but I bet she will wear sweats if we buy them for her." The administrator suggested, "She should join the track team. I think she would be a good thrower." Another student was struggling because a parent had brain cancer. Another student was "zoning out" in some classes, but not in others. Every conversation about a student was about support.

For the fifteen most at-risk freshmen, "trifold interventions" are developed. In conjunction with the "Data Guru" in the district, teachers compile evidence of a student's record, including absences, office referrals, GPA, test scores, parental contacts, and school information. This is the first side of the trifold. In the middle are steps that need to be taken to improve performance. The final side is the side where the student and parent/guardian agree to particular steps. These trifold interventions served as communication, support, and accountability.

The Open Program

One particular example of this is the "Open Program." In 2012 to 2013, a leadership team of fifteen teachers and administrators began meeting on Fridays after school for the entire year. As a team, they decided to do an open project-based course. A member of the team described the development of the course:

> We were originally thinking about science. We looked at recycling to reduce waste that the school was producing. We looked at logistics, and it did not work that way. We were looking at sophomores, but the science was too open for what they could take. We looked at math and English and were trying to come up with a SIP (School Improvement Plan) for the next century. It seemed as if with the full leadership team there were too many chefs. Two of us got together, and we created a schematic for this.

The Open Program was for honors math and English Language Arts (ELA) students in their sophomore year. The first semester, thirteen students took accelerated math and ELA and then spent two hours and fifteen minutes per day during their second semester working on projects of their choosing that meet Common Core State Standards in math and ELA. For example, one student built an online stoichiometry calculator that, according to his teacher, "was better than anything else available online." The student, who did not know how to code before the project, earned an internship as a website analyst because of this work. All thirteen students continued into their junior year to Open Program Passions, where they developed passion portfolios, including interviews, resumes, scholarships, college essays, and job shadowing. Additionally, the juniors served as mentors for the sophomores. Through survey and grade data, students report higher satisfaction with school and similar grades to comparable students. Teachers were energized by the program development and student work. One educator said, "I remember leaving meetings on an endorphin high."

3.4 WHAT CAN WE DO RIGHT NOW?

Now that you have read about examples like the freshmen team and the Open Program, what kinds of changes to the design of teachers' work needs to happen at your school?

What needs to change about the design of administrators' work?

How might this affect students' work?

DEVELOPMENT ACTIVITIES AND EXPERIENCES

How does a small school with limited resources and limited opportunities for collaboration even think about leadership development opportunities? Out of necessity, development has to be about the leadership work. There is no practice to lead or simulated leadership. Development means leading with others.

One unsuccessful initiative was instructive. As part of their data teams, groups of teachers worked with a program called "Rigorous Curriculum Design" (RCD). While there was training of teacher leaders and a committee to make course adjustments to implementation, teachers perceived the program as a top-down mandate that did not help students. Teachers received one to two early release days per month to work on the templates. According to administrators, teachers described the RCD templates as "a bunch of Mickey Mouse BS."

This is more than an example of a lack of teacher buy-in. "Buy-in" implies that there is a program that needs to be sold to teachers. Certainly, teachers were not sold on RCD. But the lack of successful implementation goes deeper than lack of buy-in. The

RCD initiative did not tap the teacher expertise in the building. Teachers were not opposed to rigorous curriculum design or collaborating. They were opposed to templates, hoops, and reporting requirements that they did not believe improved their teaching. In a school where teachers lead and have discretion over their own development, RCD seems out of place.

Teachers were not opposed to rigorous curriculum design or collaborating. They were opposed to templates, hoops, and reporting requirements that did not improve their teaching.

The development activities and experiences that were changing practice were connected to the SIP. The reason for their success was the shared vision that they represented. Remember, the SIP was written by administrations, teachers, and students and built on the specific strengths and needs of the community. The Freshmen Team, the Open Program, Club 9, and even community service were all represented in the SIP. The experience of collaboratively writing the SIP with administrators, teachers, and students was a development experience. The work of the fifteen-person leadership team that generated the idea for the Open Program was development. The implementation of Club 9 and moving the program through appropriate legal and administrative requirements was a meaningful development experience. Collecting survey data from students about the effect of the Open Program is an opportunity for course correction, refinement, and growth. Freshmen Team meetings where student assets and challenges are discussed develops leadership.

Most importantly, there is a culture that allows students and teachers to bring their own ideas forward for ways to improve the school. One teacher described administrators' approach to teacher leadership development. "The hands-off approach to leadership development sometimes forces us to develop ourselves as leaders." Most of the collaboration around new experiences and activities begins as informal conversations among teachers. In my observations, I noted three teachers who were the primary connectors and catalysts for these ideas. All three were effective educators first. Students were their priorities. They were constantly seeking new opportunities to improve the educational experiences of their students. This drive led them to seek out colleagues who could partner with them in their work. Every example of successful leadership development I found in this school occurred because of teachers and/or students seeking out others to solve a problem. Early in the process, they sought administrative input and support, and together, the initiative emerged.

Of course, in a small school, some development opportunities have to occur beyond the school and district. One teacher succinctly summarized the challenge of finding content-specific development opportunities. "Because our school is so small, we have to go out and find some of it (development opportunities) on our own. I am trying to get the other two math teachers into a math network, but they both have kids so they are very busy." Additionally, teachers did not report any development opportunities for administrators to learn to work with teacher leaders beyond the collaboration that was already occurring.

While the school does face some leadership development challenges for teachers and administrators, they are attempting to develop student leadership in meaningful ways. For a number of years, the school has hosted a basketball game for the special education students that the entire school attends and the varsity basketball players officiate. One teacher described the impact of the leadership development.

> So, what I noticed one year when I was watching was that we had a few kids who I would have considered at-risk who were typically the class clowns. They were not really interested in academics, but they worked really well with that population of students. They really excelled in that leadership role, and I was flabbergasted.

> So, we have been in the planning stage for about a year. Next week we start piloting the program where we have a couple of students taking that leadership role. We have a student from the Open Program who is interested in going into special education who is helping to develop curriculum for this as part of her Open Program project. She bounces ideas off of us. We give her feedback, and suggest time frames. So, she has been instrumental in developing the curriculum.

3.5 WHAT CAN WE DO RIGHT NOW?

What have been the three most impactful leadership development experiences in your career?

- What made them impactful?

- How does your school create more of these opportunities?

What was the least impactful leadership development experience you have ever had?

- Why was it so ineffective?

- How does your school improve or eliminate these experiences?

INCREASED CAPACITY AND IMPROVED PRACTICES

Teachers and administrators attribute much of their success to the informal leadership development opportunities that occur through collaborative work. All six NBCTs cite the influence of other NBCTs in their improved teaching practice. They even talk about going through the process in "cohorts," consisting of one to two other teachers at a time. All of the NBCTs as well as other teachers with whom they work believe that they are better, more reflective teachers and leaders because of the process.

The Freshmen Team is a good example of increased capacity and improved practices. Another teacher described the impact of the Freshmen Team this way:

They [several teachers] just created that team to see that freshmen do well and succeed. They are overcoming those barriers to success: For example, they say if students get F's during their freshman year the percentage of them graduating is much less; so, they are making sure that they are more successful during freshman year.

Because the team meets regularly, they are increasing their capacity through more effective communication and coordination, which leads to improved instructional practices and support.

Based on the perceptions of both administrators and teachers, collective leadership capacity is increasing and is creating tangible results. This increased capacity included more than just teachers and administrators. One administrator highlighted the work of the school counselor.

She is the one who takes the lead for our schoolwide community service days because community service is one of our school improvement goals. She sets the meetings, she sets the agenda, she makes sure that these things get done, and then she updates me. After working through this for the last few years, this is something that she completely owns and there is no need for me to play micromanager. I am a bad micromanager. I don't do it well.

STUDENT OUTCOMES

What difference does this work make for students? While it is always difficult to isolate causal factors for student outcomes there is evidence that some leadership development is working for students.

* According to the principal, when he arrived in 2008 to 2009 as an assistant principal, there were 125 F's in a cohort of approximately 150 freshmen. "With the research showing how pivotal freshman year was—that ninth-grade experience is going to determine how that student will do. The Freshmen Team was created." The team identified the fifteen highest risk non-IEP (**Individualized Education Program)** students. They created a teacher-student

mentoring system and a homework-support system where
once-a-week students stay after school and work with
their mentors on their homework. Students have bus
transportation home. By the 2012 to 2013 school year, the
freshman class went from receiving 125 F's to seven.

- The art teacher described the more qualitative impact of
  the Freshmen Team. "They set a tone for how students are
  acculturated. This spreads beyond that team and affects all
  levels of students. Instructionally, they are leaders."
- That influence spread in other tangible ways. Since 2008 to
  2009, Advanced Placement (AP) class offerings have more
  than doubled. An administrator attributed that growth to
  one of the AP teachers. "She (the AP teacher) has made
  sure that teachers are getting the support they need to be
  successful."
- Beyond just academic outcomes, the student culture of
  the school is changing. Students are taking on leadership
  responsibilities through the Open Program, through
  community service, and in developing the SIP.
- Some of this impact is intangible—just a feeling you get
  when you walk in the school. The school was shrinking
  in size and sits in an economically depressed community.
  I walked by many empty rooms, reminders of a more
  prosperous past. However, the feeling in the building and in
  classrooms was hopeful.
  - I observed a masterful class discussion on *The Lord of the
    Flies* that made me want to return to my own freshman
    year.
  - I saw groups of students preparing for a musical that
    night that will likely be a community event.
  - From AP calculus to AP art history, I saw students
    engaged in meaningful discussions and deep learning.
    I am convinced that this was a much richer learning
    environment for students because of the leadership work
    that is occurring.
- The SIP team developed new tools to track student outcome
  data. At four different points during the school year, they
  are collecting student survey data on the school climate.
  Students responded to probes about whether or not their
  opinions were respected; if they felt safe and cared about; if

3.6 WHAT CAN WE DO RIGHT NOW?

What leadership work at your school is the most beneficial to your students?

- How do you know?

- What other feedback do you need to collect to determine the effectiveness of the work?

- How can you collect those data in a meaningful way without it being burdensome?

they were part of the school community; and if there were adults who believed in them. On nearly every measure, 80 percent or more of students responded affirmatively.

FEEDBACK LOOPS

Learning communities that are engaged in improvement depend on feedback loops (Bryk, Gomez, Grunow, & LeMahieu, 2015). Because most of the leadership work was tied to the SIP, data was constantly collected for annual review. That review was not conducted by administrators alone. It was not conducted by only teachers and administrators. The review occurred with administrators, teachers, and students. Most importantly, the ideas of all members of the school community were assessed. The school climate survey was an excellent example of this work. This was not an external audit. This was the work that occurred organically to meet the needs of a particular context. Each year programs changed to better connect the leadership assets of the school with the needs of the school community.

For example, the school just developed a "Profile Index" for each student. The idea originated with the band director and tracked how each individual student was performing with GPA, missing assignments, community service, behavior, and leadership. The index was color coded from green to red and tracked a student's progress from the point that he or she enrolled at the high school. Administrators, teachers, and students have access to this index through their learning management system.

The Open Program is another excellent example of how the school adapts to students' needs. According to the teachers in the program,

> We make sure that the project has a community emphasis. The community gets to see the kids create this when students present to community members with expertise in a particular area—forensics, leadership, athletics, and a coded stoichiometry calculator. The student did not know how to code when he started. He got an internship with a website analyst out of his work.

Originally, the Open Program was available only to sophomores. Based on data that standardized test scores were strong relative to similar students at the school who were not part of the program, survey data of students, and Open student engagement in their work, they extended the program to junior year where they can continue to develop their own ideas with teacher support. According to survey data, students in the Open program gave significantly more positive responses to probes like, "Failure is an opportunity for growth" than similar students in traditional programs.

The Open Program is not the point. Feedback and the response to feedback is the point. In a healthy school environment, leadership work addresses needs, and capitalizes on strengths. Small rural schools often get overlooked when researchers, policymakers, and practitioners look for solutions. That is a mistake we should not continue to make.

GRASSROOTS LEADERSHIP DEVELOPMENT

At a school this small, it is difficult to separate enacted leadership and leadership development. There are a limited number of leaders and a very small pool of potential followers. The resources are extremely limited and are, in fact, shrinking. Certainly, this constrains leadership development. Imagine what could be done with additional resources:

- The Open Program could be expanded to additional students.
- Instead of just a Freshmen Team, there could be support for all levels.
- Teachers could have additional time to collaborate across schools or virtually.
- The bold ideas of teachers, students, and administrators could receive the funding that would allow them to flourish.

Out of necessity, the leadership work dictates the leaders and precipitates the development needs. Due to supportive district and building administrators who lead by trying to support ideas that come from the classroom, teachers and students own the work that is occurring. The challenges this creates for coherence are real, but through the leadership of administrators, teachers, and students, the ideas that arise from inside and outside the classroom are captured and assessed. While the school will continue to deal with a shrinking student population, the leadership development that is occurring will continue to attempt to meet shifting challenges and capitalize on the unique strengths of their school community.

Chapter Review: What Matters Most for Schools (and in This Chapter)?

❖ State leaders can identify strong school leadership.

❖ District leaders, especially those with offices in trailers in school parking lots, support leadership development.

❖ Educators with the greatest capacity for leadership view leadership as about the work, not the person.

❖ Leadership development includes paraprofessionals and students.

❖ Small schools require individual leaders to develop many forms of leadership.

❖ In many cases, the leadership work of administrators, teachers, and students becomes development.

❖ Some of the best leadership development occurs when teachers and students identify needs and develop solutions together.

❖ Even when a school is shrinking, it can continue to grow.

Action Steps

1. Identify three ideas from teachers or students that need your support.

2. Identify the types of support those ideas need and determine how you can increase support for those ideas.

3. Think creatively about how these opportunities can be expanded to more teachers and students—this can be within the school, beyond the school, or virtually.

4. Determine how these ideas fit into the SIP, or whatever type of acronym or plan you use to plan and assess improvement. If the ideas fit the SIP, that is great. If not, determine if the SIP needs to change.

CHAPTER 4

The Urban Transition

"Why do you want to study us?"

M aybe this would be the typical response of any number of school leaders dealing with the challenges that exist in many urban contexts. Maybe the response is because the school conditions survey just ranks them as "average." But maybe it is because it takes a long time to recover from your school struggling so much that all thirteen of your administrators got fired. Seven years and an entirely new administrative team may not be long enough to erase the residue of the stigma attached to a failing school.

Whatever the case, this was the response of the principal of the urban high school I selected to study. The school rose to my attention based on data from the 5Essentials survey, and because it was the only high school in a large district to have a rating of "average implementation" for effective leaders and collaborative teachers. None of the other high schools in the district had ratings that were even this high.

When I pulled up to the school, there was a banner proudly displayed on the corner of the school announcing national recognition for its positive school culture. Entering the building, I was greeted by a friendly dean's assistant who took my ID, made a visitor's badge, and directed me to the office. The end of the day was near, and the halls were empty.

I met the principal in the main office. What immediately struck me about him was the fact that he seemed more like an

The Urban High School Profile (Numbers are approximate to maintain anonymity):

Total Enrollment: >1900

Instructional Spending Per Pupil: approximately $6,000

Low-Income Students: >75%

English Learners: >15%

Students with Disabilities: >10%

Graduation Rate: >77%

Ready for College: >20%

5Essentials School Environment:

    Effective Leaders: Average Implementation

    Collaborative Teachers: Average Implementation

elementary school principal than the principal of a comprehensive high school of nearly 2,000 students. He projected the warmth of an elementary principal probably because that was his position prior to becoming principal at this school. I listened carefully to catch what he was saying as he walked me back to his office, introducing me to the office staff along the way. Less than a decade ago, after serving for six years as an elementary principal, he was a parent of a senior at the school, and in his first year as an assistant principal at another high school in the district. When he heard in February that all thirteen administrators were fired, two thoughts went through his head, "Maybe that needed to happen; and I feel sorry for whoever has to take that over." That is when he got the call from the superintendent asking him to take over.

The administrative team remained in place for the rest of that school year. Needless to say, there was a high level of toxicity throughout the school and staff when he started in the fall. Although thirteen administrators were fired, he was only allowed to hire nine administrators. The principal recalled, "That was the hardest year of my life."

Although the school now experienced a far more positive culture than seven years prior, events still occurred from time to time that threatened the more stable climate and served as a reminder of the past. While the school felt safe during every one of my visits, the principal shared an example of an event that occurred a week before my first visit.

I have lots of roles. One role will be today at the faculty meeting. I do think that when I address the faculty, I perform a corporate role. I don't know if you heard about our traumatic events on Friday. It was the worst thing that could have happened. Some students wanted to hold a walkout because the auto class was not running next year. We got word of it (the walkout), and I told the kids, "Hey, we are going to send you to class, but if you meet me in the aisle area, I will talk to whoever is concerned about this."

Well, a kid pulled the fire alarm, which cleared out the building. We got kids to go back into the building, except for about 300 who decided to hold a protest. They walked around the building and right about that time when they got to the front of the building fights just broke out all over the place. There were probably six fights, and chaos everywhere, and kids running everywhere. People were videotaping everything and posting on Facebook. It was the worst. It was really traumatic, actually. And the fights had nothing to do with the auto class. Just ten kids who were bent on being destructive as soon as they got the opportunity—and then, we had kids coming onto campus who were not even our kids jumping into fights, so it was just a mess.

So yesterday, for example, I addressed the whole school in second period. I read a statement about the incident, so basically, I feel like I have a role that way, influencing people corporately. But then I think I have a role with the administrative team, because they are all leading and so my role is with the administrative team leading. I have a role with the whole PLC structure—with the PLC leaders, with the PLC advisory. So, it's working with smaller groups of teachers to try to provide structures and figure out "what to do next" strategies and structure.

This explanation of his role in working through a traumatic event was indicative of his view of leadership. He served a role in the work, but the solutions were in the work of various teams with overlapping responsibilities.

4.1 WHAT CAN WE DO RIGHT NOW?

Whether your school is urban, suburban, or rural, you face challenges that are specific to your context. What challenges are most pressing at your school?

- Have everyone on your leadership team rank the top three challenges your school faces.
- List all of the challenges and group them if possible.

- Place tally marks or "dot down" (round, colored stickers) to represent the most recurring issues.
- Identify the most pressing issue.

What leadership work is occurring to address the most pressing issue?

What leadership development needs to occur to address the issue?

ADMINISTRATIVE SUPPORT

The administrative team was not composed of charismatic leaders who will ever be featured in dramatic movies or books on school turnaround. However, the designated leader operated like a savvy elementary principal. I sat in on four different leadership teams where administrators, teachers, parents, and students met to address challenges. Administrators were involved in every team, but most of the time, they were facilitators or participants. In several instances, the principal allowed me to meet with leadership teams with no administrators present so that teachers felt free to be transparent. Almost without exception, teachers, students, and parents described the principal as "caring" and "someone we respected because he respects us."

In the Professional Learning Community (PLC) advisory meeting without any administrators, teachers shared their perspective on the principal's role in developing a vision for teacher leadership at their school that highlights the structures and ethos the principal has attempted to create.

> I think he plays a major role in how he sets that up. He has been good at wanting to have the voices of the teachers heard. He has created the structures for the teachers to generate what is happening. I hear terrible stories at other schools where if you speak your mind or say what you want to say, things come back to get you after you say what you think. That is not the case here at all. He is very open. Is he perfect at doing this? No. Are there a lot of improvements that could be made? Yes. But he definitely is genuine in wanting us to have a say.

Teachers report a high level of relational trust between themselves and the administration, and the principal in particular. As we walked down the hallways this was evident. In typical principal fashion, he has an awareness of any debris in the hallway and is almost compulsive in picking it up, but he is also aware of all of his teachers and students. He greeted and was greeted by students and teachers alike—and he always used their names.

Although the relational trust is high, particularly given where the school was seven years ago, there are perceived gaps in administrative support. When asked, "On a scale of 0 to 10 (0 representing 'absolutely nothing' and 10 representing 'everything'), how much do you know about what is happening in classrooms in your school?" the principal responded, "8.5." When I asked PLC leaders this question in their meeting in relation to any administrators, the estimate was much lower. A teacher leader shared,

> I feel like "0." He used to come in my room all the time. One year, he came in 40 times. I told him, "You used to come in my room all the time." It seems like their responsibilities have just become insane. I think I should do more of saying, "Hey, I am doing something really cool. I think you should come in."

Teachers and administrators expressed frustration over their perception of limited administrative support and lack of shared vision from the district office. This high school is located in a large urban district, and the district office is sometimes perceived as a hindrance to school-level leadership efforts. While school leaders, both teachers and administrators, cited district administrators they trusted, the majority of the frustration arose from what seemed to be constantly shifting priorities and structures. One teacher shared, "We are lacking the systemic structure—we have the flavor of the year—class visits, mentors, coming down from the district." A PLC chair reiterated, "There is not a unified vision for the whole building. When you have departments in different stages, that is hard. Now that the district wants us to do something as a department, it is hard to do the building things." In the PLC advisory meeting, there was consensus that "District office initiatives keep getting pushed down. Until we are the authority for what happens in the schools, we can't really do much. How do we get time to be leaders?"

> *"District office initiatives keep getting pushed down. Until we are the authority for what happens in the schools, we can't really do much. How do we get time to be leaders?"*

These frustrations are certainly not unique to this school or district. In fact, these frustrations are common refrains from teachers and administrators, particularly in large, urban districts. The district office is often seen as the enemy of autonomy, and the "other" that does not understand the realities of the classroom or a particular school context. Contrast this with the rural district office in the trailer of the high school parking lot in Chapter 3. That district is less than sixty miles away. Certainly, both districts have challenges and opportunities, but this is why equifinality— many ways to reach the same goal—is so important.

Context matters.

A lot.

The principal and administrative teams at the two high schools are not that different philosophically. Both genuinely want teachers to develop, implement, and analyze their own solutions to challenges. Both want teachers to lead from their strengths. Both want to involve teachers, students, and the community in leadership work. However, the constraints on their own support of leadership development are very different. In the urban high school, trust is very fragile, and it has taken seven years for the administrative team to build that trust. As you will see, that trust is still very tenuous. The school does have PLCs, something that is much easier than it was in the rural school, but they face challenges. Trying to maintain a steady focus on improvement efforts at the school level is difficult when district administration is mandating new initiatives each year. A coherent vision can be difficult to maintain even after it has been developed, if the perception is that the vision is subordinate to the whims of the district office.

> *A coherent vision can be difficult to maintain even after it has been developed, if the perception is that the vision is subordinate to the whims of the district office.*

CAPACITY

When interviewed, teachers revealed perceptions of leadership capacity among teachers and administrators that were fairly typical. Several teacher leaders shared their perspectives:

> English teacher: You have people who are spread very thin because they want to be very involved in so many types of school leadership. You have other people who are very involved with students. Most people are not both. There

4.2 WHAT CAN WE DO RIGHT NOW?

On a scale of 1 to 10, what is your school's relationship like with the district office?

1 = "The district office is the enemy of progress."

10 = "The district office is a tremendous support to our school's leadership work."

| 1 | 2 | 3 | 4 | 5 | 6 | 7 | 8 | 9 | 10 |

Are responses from teachers and administrators on your team similar or different?

What might be three next steps to either build or solidify district office connections?

isn't anything that someone else can do to engage them.... There is always a reason someone can't help. I have two young kids; I know I am taking time away from them, but it [leadership] is a priority for me.

PLC leader: I am tapped out. It boils down to teacher comfort—you don't want to throw someone into a leadership position if they don't want to take it. Many teachers are comfortable and want to stay within their boundaries. Currently, we are in limbo about PLCs, so I am a little unsure of where we are at. It is a little discouraging.

These comments are common across schools. Identified teacher leaders add, add, and add. Because they are close to students and other colleagues, they are the most likely to recognize needs. They continue to try to meet those needs sometimes to the point of burnout or to the detriment of other professional or personal aspirations (Eckert, Ulmer, Khatchatryan, & Ledesma, 2016). Administrators know that these leaders will get things done and they continue to return to them. Conversely, people who do not aspire to lead are sometimes tapped to lead by default. One PLC leader shared this sentiment. "I am the PLC leader because no one else will do it. I don't think we are cultivating leaders.

I wasn't picked because I am doing a bang-up job in the classroom." This honesty communicated the frustration that exists in systems where power is perceived to reside elsewhere. Initiatives are "done" to teachers instead of "with" or "by" them. This creates a cultural lawnmower for grassroots leadership. This cultural lawnmower results in comments like this from a PLC leader: "I don't talk a lot. I don't want to say the wrong things. I don't want anyone to feel that I know more than they do."

> *Initiatives are "done" to teachers instead of "with" or "by" them. This creates a cultural lawnmower for grassroots leadership.*

According to teachers, there was untapped potential at the high school. The key is to allow the work to dictate who leads. A social studies teacher highlighted this issue. "There is probably some untapped potential. The ones who are leading—they are doing as much as they can with PBIS (positive behavior intervention supports), PLCs, and Universal Team. There are people out there that could be used."

Another veteran teacher offered a solution: "There are a lot of talented teachers here. If I were principal, I would get a lot of younger teachers leading and get people like myself off of things. There are a handful of teachers constantly doing everything."

The principal sees capacity in his teachers and is very positive about his administrative team. However, he sees a "mixed bag" of functional and dysfunctional PLCs. When asked to quantify this, he identified approximately 25 percent of the PLCs at the school as functioning well.

> I do think there is teacher leadership, but I think the teacher leadership happens more informally. I think that the PBIS structure has leveraged some teacher leadership. I think that the PLCs have a mixed bag of leadership. Some teachers are acting as leaders and some are not. Some are actually acting as leadership working against school goals.

Some teachers may have leadership capacity, but we must be careful to avoid the presumption that all leadership is good (Kellerman, 2004; Lieberman & Miller, 2004; Murphy, 2005). The needed work determines the leadership, but a shared vision should precede the work. The PLCs are a classic example. The

4.3 WHAT CAN WE DO RIGHT NOW?

If you have PLCs or some other collaborative structure for leadership at your school, how are they working?

If some PLCs are working better than others, what could you do to spread their effectiveness?

Where is there more leadership capacity in your school? Could PLCs help identify and build that capacity? If so, how?

What other vehicles are available for building capacity in your school?

capacity for effective, collective leadership is determined by the shared vision of the necessary work. Not all leaders share this vision and therefore lack capacity. The leaders at the school must determine the needed work; identify the people already doing the work; welcome others to the work; and with them, decide how to build capacity to improve the work.

CONDITIONS AND RESOURCES

The school culture, structures, politics, and resources are very closely related to leadership capacity. Similar to the rural high school, teachers believe that there is an open-door policy with administrators. Most teachers interviewed said they felt comfortable talking to administrators, but that most information was shared via email. One teacher said, "Administration has our back. I think it is an open line of communication. The principal and AP (assistant principal) have open doors. It is generally positive both ways."

While trust of school administration is relatively high, teacher leaders estimate that trust among teachers is an issue for 20 to

30 percent of the staff. Most teachers are comfortable with other teachers observing them teach and giving feedback. However, some fear that this observation might somehow be part of the evaluation process.

Many school-level decisions about resource allocation and problem solving have been made in recent years through collaborative efforts. A couple of tangible results are representative.

Physical Changes

School violence used to be significantly more prevalent at this school; I observed several team meetings focused on school safety and discipline. Teachers, students, parents, and administrators were meeting to discuss how to improve school culture. Two of the tangible results of this kind of problem-solving were a wall extension and a koi pond.

The main entrance to the school is directly across from the cafeteria. When students enter the building, there is a brick wall that rises about halfway up to a fifteen-foot high ceiling that separates the entrance from the cafeteria.

The wall used to be about eight feet long. More fights.

It is now forty feet long. Fewer fights.

Why did the change matter?

A team of leaders identified the hot spot for fights as just past the end of the eight-foot wall between the entrance and the cafeteria. Students would enter the school in the morning or at lunchtime when large numbers of students were in the cafeteria, and fights would ensue where there was a large audience. In order to reduce the possibility of an audience for fights as soon as students entered the building, the wall was extended to the end of the cafeteria.

On the other side of the cafeteria was a courtyard. In order to create a more peaceful environment, resources were allocated to build a koi pond that serves as a type of an outdoor classroom. Financial resources dedicated to this project have paid dividends in school pride and created a different atmosphere in one of the most challenging parts of the building.

Obviously, the wall extension and the koi pond did not solve school problems on their own. School leadership altered entry and exit patterns at the school and increased lunch supervision, and school culture was more positive in general. However, the physical changes did make a difference and were tangible reminders of how the school was changing.

The PLC Site Exception

Time is always a scarce resource. Interestingly, some of the time crunch that teachers feel is often of their own making.

One of the first meetings I observed was a PLC leader meeting with more than twenty educators. They were discussing what to do after a vote the previous week about a site exception. This school was voting on getting a site exception to continue to get early release days the following year for PLC meetings. For the previous two years, the school had one early release day per month for PLC work. Due to limited progress, the PLC leaders proposed that they move to weekly early release or no early release at all. As one teacher said, "We need to go all in or we will continue to tread water." In order to get weekly early release time, a site exception to the collectively bargained contract was needed. Demonstrating a commitment to PLCs, over 74 percent of the faculty voted to move to weekly time. This was a sign of tremendous progress relative to where the school culture was seven years before.

However, the site exception required 75 percent of teachers to vote for the weekly PLC time. The site exception failed by one vote. The following year there would not be early release time for PLCs.

The conversation that ensued in the meeting offered insight into school conditions. Repeatedly teachers said that for some teachers "the contract was king." For some teachers, if the work was not described in the contract, it did not get done. Some of the 26 percent who voted against PLCs thought that they might be able to rid themselves of common assessments and what they perceived as "top-down mandates from the district." One PLC leader appraised the situation in the meeting.

> The biggest issue is that people thought that this would end PLC because they thought this would now be outside of the contractual day. It has nothing to do with you personally [the principal]. It had to do with so many people who are "so contractual." With that idea—that this would circumvent district mandates—people thought that by voting "no" they don't have to do this.

Undaunted, the principal shared his belief that PLCs could continue. He would pay for substitutes for teams that were interested in continuing to meet with Title I money that he could use for professional development. In a separate interview, an English teacher confirmed that the principal would make resources available whenever possible. "I usually go and ask for time. He would give you money from his wallet to pay for a sub."

This uncertainty about PLCs posed challenges for the leadership structure at the school. An English teacher described the process for how decisions are made and disseminated at the school.

> PLCs' advisory makes decisions that are passed to PLC leaders and then to PLCs. I would like to think that structure would be in place, but we are not sure. Having discussions about curriculum is important and valuable. I know we will go back as a PLC leader and look at SIP (School Improvement Plan). I have been on SIP a long time. It was never a collaboration with colleagues. It is more like that now. With a PLC structure in place, it is more collaborative than it has ever been. When you look at those numbers, three-fourths of the teachers really believe in it.

The PLC vote was indicative of the trust issues that remain at the school. While there is trust of building administration, there is often a lack of trust of district administration. An English teacher described the situation. "The district has cut us off at the knees. We had some good things in place and then the district changed things on us. We had developed our own assessments, but then the district said we have to do the same assessments in every grade in every class in the district." This response led some potential leaders to avoid moving beyond their classrooms because they do not feel that they have the power to enact solutions that they believe are necessary.

Interestingly, one year after the original vote, 84 percent of the teachers voted for the site exception to have weekly PLC time. Progress.

WORK DESIGN

Part of the PLC vote is related to the design of the work at the school. An English teacher attributed the vote to "singletons"—teachers who were the only teachers of particular classes. "Some of that 25 percent [who voted against expanding PLC time in the first vote] are the singletons. For them, PLC time is stupid. How could they collaborate with people from other buildings? That might change things." Even in a school this large, personal learning networks needed to expand beyond the walls of the school.

Like most high schools, this school depended on department chairs to provide leadership. Interviews with many of the department chairs and PLC leaders revealed that most saw the school moving in a positive trajectory. They cited having better conversations about assessment and student learning, but they hoped for more. An interchange between the principal and a PLC leader about collaboration was indicative of the tension between where the school was and where leaders would like it to be.

PLC Leader: "I am maxed out for [professional development] courses. I read every book out there. I wanted lesson study ten years ago. We have been doing some great stuff—that has been deep-sixed. I am kind of agitated. I want to do lesson study—how can we ever do that?

Principal: "I don't think this conversation is hinging on whether we do lesson study. I think that is PLC 401 and we are probably at PLC 101."

PLC Leader: "It comes up now like it is a new idea. There is no time to do lesson study."

The PLC leader wanted to go deeper with his colleagues through lesson study. Lesson study required common planning, reciprocal observation, and significant time for data collection and reflection. The work of the school was not designed in such a way to make that possible.

Much of the work of leaders and committees revolved around school safety considerations. A majority of one meeting of administrators was following up on the work of the Safety and Discipline Committee (a contractually required committee of administrators and teachers). The topics addressed included:

- Ticketing for parking
- AM food rules
- Jaywalking
- Roaming the halls at 8th period
- Disrespect in the halls
- Elevator congestion
- Hall monitor gathering
- Dropping off students without a pass

These were not trivial issues. The majority of office referrals and behavioral issues in the school occurred in the hallways. Administrators attributed many of the issues to hallway congestion. When students congregate in the halls, individual teachers have trouble moving groups of students, arguments happen, students are late to class, or they "bring drama" into the classroom. Nearly ten minutes of the administrators meeting was devoted to determining how to reduce traffic around the elevators.

Another insight that the principal shared was their need to effectively use their ability to search students when they enter the building. On rare occasions, police dropped students off at the school, and when school officials searched these students they would occasionally find drugs or weapons. The principal explained, "The police were not negligent. We have more rights to search students without cause than they do."

These conversations were a far cry from lesson study. To address this, the leadership teams in the school were attempting to clarify roles for the SIP team and PLC leaders. PLC leaders and department chairs aspired to greater engagement with each other around teaching and learning. Some discussed district initiatives in the past that required peer observation.

> We divided up all of the teachers and did observations. Teachers were unsure about our purpose; they wanted to be sure it was not part of the appraisal plan. We did have time to give feedback, and I think for some of them it was kind of an "aha" moment. For some it validated what they were doing. As a leader, it was helpful for me to see what was going on in other parts of the building.

Another teacher described a rich collaborative experience.

> We just had a PLC meeting. Another teacher was talking about a Kagan strategy [prevalent strategies for student collaboration]. She watched me do it. That is what you really want. It was very informal.... We just looked at data from a common assessment. It is not evaluative because who the heck am I? I am just a teacher. That was on the PPD day [one of four district professional practice days]—we spent three hours on assessment data. I spent more because I was the PLC leader, so I just sucked it up and got it done. We looked

at our scoring rubric. Did we like it? How could we talk about it with students? It was real PD (professional development).

The school and district are attempting to coordinate and sustain leadership efforts. A PLC leader described how she was selected for her overlapping roles. "I had to apply to be on the district curriculum committee. Once I was selected, I was encouraged to also lead the PLC, which had to be voted on by my peers. I think some of our success is due to understanding the school and district context for curriculum."

Complete the Collective Leadership Inventory, Part III, shown here. What kinds of things are keeping this school from getting to Collective Leadership 401 instead of remaining stuck in "PLC 101?" Are similar constraints affecting your school?

Collective Leadership Inventory, Part III	
How do conditions and resources affect the work design at your school?	
How does the work design affect conditions and resources at your school?	
What could your school do right now to alter work design that would not require any additional resources?	
What do both teachers and administrators need to do to get your school to Collective Leadership 401?	
What is your school's current Collective Leadership level?	Collective Leadership 101 ____ Collective Leadership 201 ____ Collective Leadership 301 ____ Collective Leadership 401 ____

DEVELOPMENT ACTIVITIES AND EXPERIENCES

While there are some attempts to coordinate leadership efforts between the school and district, there are very few formal opportunities for leadership development. Once again, leadership development occurs through the work of leadership teams. The strongest example of this leadership development is the PBIS Universal Team. The Universal Team addresses Tier One interventions for PBIS—interventions that impact the entire school. Perhaps not surprisingly, the Universal Team was the inspiration of a special education teacher in the building who saw a need for developing a more positive school culture. This was not a district initiative. Although the Universal Team is supported by administration, administrators do not lead the team. The principal serves as a member of the team.

Perhaps the best way to understand the team is to describe a typical meeting. Six teachers, the principal, a school security officer, a parent, and two students met in a windowless basement room of the school. The meeting began with a discussion of office referrals. What follows is a representative sample of quotations to provide a sense of the problem solving and development. Try to read the quotations with an eye for the reality of the problems and the effectiveness of this type of venue to elicit honest dialogue.

March PBIS Universal Team Meeting:

"The freshmen are killing us. They have 289 referrals in February—118 students have 289 referrals. In that same month, eighteen seniors got twenty referrals."

A teacher asked, "Is it a kid problem or a teacher problem? I have a kid I could write up every day, but I don't."

Another member of the team asked the student [a senior], "Aren't you glad you are leaving?"

She replied, "Yeah, but I don't want to leave it like this."

Another teacher pointed out, "As students get older, we are writing less referrals."

(Continued)

(Continued)

"Is that because we lose some of those students?" asked another teacher.

The student observed another challenge. "Hall monitors are walking right past and not doing anything about loitering."

A teacher added, "The hallway is almost as bad as the class-rooms for referrals. The problem is that students are friends with the hall monitors. They don't really enforce it."

Another teacher pointed out part of the challenge was that some students were wearing headphones in the hallways. "Most of the time, they won't hear you because they have headphones on in the hall. When we have to raise our voice to be heard, they think we are yelling. I am interested to hear what our students think."

A student shared, "Students think you are here to serve them. They want to be the cool kids and don't think they have to lis-ten to you."

After these attempts to fully understand the issue, the principal attempted to push the conversation toward solutions. "We can admire the problem, but what is the plan of attack? We have shown we can make improvements."

The administrator in charge of security suggested that "DAs (deans assistants) need to know about the issues in the hallway."

A teacher pushed back and said, "I have sent you emails about issues with DAs and have not gotten a response."

One teacher expressed her concern about keeping traffic mov-ing in the hallway as a single teacher. "It is a team. We need to have two people in the hallway saying it. It has to be two people saying the same thing."

Another teacher added, "We were close to giving up on the hallway until we got two or three teachers out there. Teachers have to work with each other and the DAs to get this done."

Another teacher acknowledged the challenge of balancing hallway discipline with relationships. "I think we are espe-cially here because we are trying to develop a relationship. It can become too friendly of a relationship, but this issue is important. Getting the kids moving in the hallways would solve a lot of problems."

The parent suggested, "What about an emphasis to clear the halls? Could we send an email to all of the teachers and make an announcement to the whole school that we are going to focus on clearing the halls and keeping traffic moving?"

A teacher encouraged the principal, "I think your voice would be powerful. People want to be behind you."

Moving to another topic, the team leader shared, "Jimmy John's has offered to give a student of the month award to a class. Could be a way to reward a Tier Two kid. Could we figure out how to get kids who improved?"

Another teacher suggested, "Let's ask teachers to identify the most-improved student and give us the criteria. We also need to discuss our Five-Star Menu [top-level rewards for positive behavior]."

The meeting continued for an hour with people sharing issues and possible solutions with the entire group. All voices were equally heard, and if anything, deference was given to the students. The conversation represented the kind of solution-oriented work that was improving the school. Leadership development was occurring because the work was being done by all of the people responsible for making improvements. The team was looking unblinkingly at evidence, not assigning blame, or wallowing in the problem, and respected the contributions that everyone made.

> *The team was looking unblinkingly at evidence, not assigning blame, or wallowing in the problem, and respected the contributions that everyone made.*

INCREASED CAPACITY AND IMPROVED PRACTICE

In PLCs and departments at the school where leadership is developing, the dialogue in the Universal Team meeting represents the kind of work that is occurring. In other PLCs and departments, the work feels like a mandate or something that is being done to teachers and students. Not much is happening on those teams.

Increased capacity through leadership development is leading to improved practices. Because of the success of the Universal Team and PBIS, the high school has received national recognition for their work. The school's data tells them that what they are doing is working. They are the only high school in the district with more positive rewards than referrals.

Pockets of improved practice are occurring throughout the school. Several of the PLCs are analyzing student work, planning together, dividing tasks, and improving practice together. The principal identified five of these teams, and based on my observations of the teams and their interactions, his assessment was accurate. Determining how to spread these experiences to other teams is the challenge, particularly with the tenuous nature of the time for PLCs.

STUDENT OUTCOMES

There were a number of leading indicators of improvement over the past seven years, including several programs that have improved outcomes for students.

- Students in the **Advancement Via Individual Determination** (AVID) program are finding increasing levels of success. The AVID program is a national program designed to support average students who need additional study skills, support, or mentoring to get to college. The AVID coordinator was well respected by colleagues and students alike for her ability to bring together necessary resources for students through her leadership.

- Club Adelante was formed to support English learners.
- Office referrals are down.
- Positive recognition of student behavior is up.
- An increasing number of students are returning to the high school as teachers and entering leadership positions. Their level of contextual understanding is viewed as an asset to the school.
- The number students in advanced placement (AP) and honors classes has increased significantly with raised expectations and opportunities extended to more students. This has been a challenge for the teachers of the more advanced courses. However, changing attitudes were represented by this leader's comment. "Why should AP teachers have a corner on kids who don't fail classes?" As a result of these changing attitudes, more students were taking and passing AP classes.

FEEDBACK LOOPS

One of the most challenging areas for the school is feedback. Fortunately, there appeared to be trust between teachers and administrators. The open-door policy of administrators and particularly the principal, allowed for informal feedback. In some cases, the informal feedback was more valuable than the formal feedback.

Flawed Formal Feedback

Unfortunately, aligning the vision and strategy for leadership development and school improvement with a district that is constantly shifting strategies is problematic. The district target seems to move, multiply, and change shape on an annual basis. School leaders do not feel that they have the tools to accurately collect feedback on what is working and what is not.

In the first PLC Leaders meeting I observed, the principal and assistant principal were leading the team through data analysis of a survey they administered over the past four years. The "survey" was really a rubric assessing implementation of seventeen PLC tenets, such as shared mission, vision, values, goals, culture, curriculum, and assessment. All of these tenets contribute to successful schools, but the method of data collection was creating challenges for interpretation. PLCs were asked to complete the survey by marking in quarter increments where they believe the school falls. Teams placed an "X" to represent their opinion of the school's position. For example, if they believed the school was solidly in the "initiation" stage, they might put an "X" at the second hash beyond 2 for a score of 2.5.

For the past four years, the assistant principal has collected all of these rubrics from each PLC and tabulated the results from the paper rubrics. At the end of each year, the results were compared to determine if the teams and the school were making progress. For example, "Shared vision" had a schoolwide average of 3.26 in 2016 and 3.36 in 2015, resulting in a .10 decline. In the PLC meeting, all of the tenets with lower scores from the previous year were discussed.

Unfortunately, the majority of the time was spent discussing the rubric tool, with the discussion driven by questions like these:

"How is a 3.5 different than a 3.75?"

"Is a 3.26 average really different than 3.36?"

"Is this referring to the school, our team, or the teams we know at the school?"

An hour of meeting time with over twenty educators as well as many hours of administrative time went into this well-meaning data collection process. However, the data did little to explain the challenges the school faced.

The principal articulated the feedback challenge. "We are in a really problematic place in education because there's no clear scoreboard. So, it's really easy to think that no change is needed because there is no scoreboard. And the scoreboard that we do have is not very tied to what is really going on." How has this school tracked its progress? How will this school track its progress? These are the leadership questions that should drive their work. Over seven years, leaders can point to tangible and intangible changes that represent incremental improvements. To accelerate that improvement, meaningful evidence needs to be collected, and honest conversations are essential. The Universal Team and several PLCs are at the point of relational trust between administrators and teachers. Where they go from here is determined by the leadership work they choose to tackle next.

Beneficial Formal and Informal Feedback—One Year Later

When I sent this chapter back to the principal to ensure its accuracy, he described some of the progress the school had made since my visits during the spring semester. Due to the informal feedback the school leadership teams received, they made some significant changes. He said,

> I guess I see where we are today and see how we are in such a better place. Our PLCs are healthier than they have ever been after a recent check-in on the PLC groups. This all happened without any regular release time. The credit goes to the PLC leaders. Additionally, we did some authentic work at the end of last year to identify where we went wrong in our implementation [of PLCs]. We looked at ten common mistakes [that happen with PLC implementation], and we had made all ten mistakes! However, we identified lack of clarity and communication of expectations as major issues. We did a great deal of work to define the PLC process and our expectations. I think this has led to our growth, even without release time. We just voted again [on PLC release time], and this time the weekly time passed with 84 percent of the vote.

The principal also shared data he collected from sixteen PLC leaders after the PLC changes were implemented. In less than a year, PLCs had more than tripled the common assessments they created. On three different probes related to progress, participation, and overall investment in the PLCs, leaders were significantly more positive. Teams that reported being "invested" in PLCs nearly doubled in less than a year, and all teams reported some participation by all members, which was an increase of almost 20 percent from the previous years.

This is positive feedback under almost any circumstances; however, this occurred during the year when no time had been set aside for PLCs. That makes these findings truly remarkable.

Honest conversations after the failed vote seemed to result in healthier PLCs and a positive vote.

A SCHOOL IN TRANSITION

The entire time I was at the school, I had a nagging question—what was the school like seven years ago? What would the school have felt like? Without being able to go back in time, I was dependent on the stories that people shared: school fights, faculty acrimony, and bitterness spread by administrators who had been fired yet remained in their positions for three more months.

As I walked the hallways of the school with the soft-spoken former elementary school principal, I could only imagine the transition that had occurred to get to this point. Teachers were working together with administrators and sharing challenges and opportunities openly with me. The school was a nationally recognized model for PBIS. Parents, students, and teachers were leading meetings to improve the school with the principal as a participant.

No school will ever arrive at perfect leadership. No school will ever perfectly master leadership development. Certainly, this school had not. However, the leadership development that was occurring had taken a school on the brink to a school that was filled with opportunities for growth—a school where the needed work was dictating who would lead.

Chapter Review: What Matters Most for Schools (and in This Chapter)?

- ❖ Elementary principals can be great high school leaders.

- ❖ Relational trust is essential for leadership development.

- ❖ Equifinality—many ways to reach the same goal—is even more important in challenging contexts.

- ❖ Even after it has been developed, a coherent vision can be difficult to maintain if the perception is that the vision is subordinate to the whims of the district office.

- ❖ Leadership talent, beyond the usual suspects, must be developed.

- ❖ Collective leadership development can lead to tangible solutions to problems.

- ❖ Finding time for development can be challenging when only 74 percent of the staff want it.

- ❖ Leadership must be developed and exerted on a school's most pressing needs. Sometimes, that is school safety.

- ❖ Leadership works best in teams, teams that can include students, parents, teachers, and administrators— particularly teams that look unblinkingly at evidence, do not assign blame, and respect the contributions of everyone.

- ❖ Leadership is never perfect. No school will ever perfectly master leadership development.

Action Steps

You have used the LDR tool. You know you are ready for leadership development; now you need to identify with whom you need to work.

For *Administrators and Teachers*:

1. Identify other teachers, students, parents, or administrators (district or building) you need to engage to solve a pressing issue.

2. Identify PLCs or other collaboration vehicles to share the work.

3. If they exist, identify what you need to do to break down barriers between your school and district administrators.

4. Identify allies at the district office and those people who need to become allies.

5. Let the work dictate who needs to participate in the efforts and then engage those people to increase the shared expertise of your team. When possible, include students and parents as well.

CHAPTER 5

The Suburban Blueprint

"There is a great quote from Mike Tyson, 'Everybody's got a plan until they get punched in the mouth.'"

The temperature was just above freezing. There was some mix of rain, snow, and ice all coming down at the same time. It was 7:03 AM. This was classic Chicago weather for March. A student was walking into the school about fifteen feet ahead of me. I am not sure how my existence penetrated the fog that typically surrounds teenagers at that time of the morning, but he stopped and held the door open for me.

When I entered the front office, the school secretary was managing students, staff, and parents with an easy calm. As I walked the hallways of the school with the principal on my way to several PLC meetings, I smelled breakfast wafting down the hall. It was math and science departments' turn to provide the monthly breakfast for the entire staff. My mood on entering the school had somewhat matched the weather. As I crossed the threshold into the school, everything just felt better.

If you have spent much time in schools, you know the feeling. I notice it most in elementary schools—there is hopefulness and energy. When I remember schools like this, my memory seems to make them a little brighter than they probably were. When I walked into this school, it felt like the high school version of that memory. I arrived on a late start Wednesday that happens every

The Suburban High School Profile (Numbers are approximate to maintain anonymity):

Total Enrollment: >2100

Instructional Spending Per Pupil: approximately $7,500

Low-Income Students: >25%

English Learners: <5%

Students with Disabilities: >10%

Graduation Rate: >90%

Ready for College: >70%

5Essentials School Environment:
Effective Leaders: More Implementation
Collaborative Teachers: More Implementation

other week for the first seventy-five minutes of the day. Some students were working quietly in groups in the commons area outside the office, but most wouldn't come until later. There was an energy in the PLC meetings that seemed almost unnatural at 7:30 in the morning as teachers engaged in deeply professional conversations about standards-based grading, lab innovations, student work, and what to do about retakes.

THE THIRTY-MINUTE TEACHER-LED STAFF MEETING

A month later, I returned for a monthly staff meeting. It was a testing day that sounded like typical education acronym insanity—PARCC (Partnership for Assessment of Readiness for College and Careers), ACT (American College Testing), and PLAN (one of ACT's suite of tests) were scheduled for that day. The cafeteria was filled with over 200 educators. The meeting began with a round of applause for "making it through the day." The school's vision statement was on a screen behind the principal. The basic premise of the vision statement is to inspire students to become lifelong learners. But before he read the vision statement, as he does at the beginning of every faculty meeting, he said, "There are only a few things that we can control. Today was one of those days where you have to fake it until you make it. The reason it goes off without a hitch is because of the work that you guys do." Then he cited the Mike Tyson quotation from the beginning of this chapter. I wondered to myself how many times, if ever, Mike Tyson was used as the inspiration at the beginning of a school staff meeting. I am guessing not many. However, this was not the typical school or school leadership team.

The monthly staff meeting lasted thirty minutes. I have spent over twenty years teaching and have never been in a staff meeting that lasted thirty minutes. The principal spoke for a total of four minutes thirty-two seconds. The choir and orchestra teacher updated the staff on their trip with 150 students to China for eleven days and five performances. Two counselors shared about their plan for school and community pride built around social emotional learning goals and focusing on six areas—hallways, classrooms, cafeteria/commons, physical education, electronics, and school events. Another teacher shared about students' need to earn community service hours starting with a freshman transition experience. A summer reading program for teachers and staff was announced. The faculty selection was *Drive* by Daniel Pink. Two "muggings" occurred. A "mugging" consisted of a tongue-in-cheek gift of a mug to an educator as recognition of quality work. Other teachers acknowledged the efforts of the orchestra and choir director, and they were presented with mugs. The athletic director announced an upcoming lunch provided by the athletic department, and then the meeting was over. Two additional observations from my month in the school: 1) Teachers clapped for every colleague who came to the front to speak, and 2) The school builds community by sharing meals.

According to the 5Essentials surveys, this suburban high school has a relatively high level of effective leadership and collaboration among teachers. Of the three high schools I studied, this school had the highest ratings for leadership, collaboration, and student outcomes. I was curious to know if this was a function of its suburban demographics or if there was truly something different occurring that could be replicated. Looking at school data, I could rule out the notion that it was just additional financial resources. The district spends right around the national average per pupil and a similar amount to the schools in the two previous chapters. What is working at this school?

5.1 WHAT CAN WE DO RIGHT NOW?

Each school context is different, so monthly thirty-minute teacher-led staff meetings may not work everywhere.

What is the ideal frequency of staff meetings at your school? (Circle one)

Daily

Weekly

Monthly

Quarterly

Annually

What is the ideal length of a staff meeting for your school? (Circle one)

15 minutes

30 minutes

45 minutes

1 hour

2 hours

All day

Who should lead the staff meeting? (Circle one)

Teachers

Administrators

Both teachers and administrators

Now look at the way teachers and administrators responded to these questions.

- Are the responses similar or different?
- If there are differences, or there appears to be a need for a change from your current staff meeting structure, what needs to change?

- What type of feedback is needed to determine if these changes are improving your work together?

ADMINISTRATIVE SUPPORT

Teachers still talk about the first meeting the current principal held two years earlier. Before the school year started, the principal lined the hallways with students involved in athletics and activities, and he had the band play as the teachers walked through the building. "We did not know about it. They just cheered and clapped for us. It was like a cheerleading team for the teachers." The boost to morale was palpable. When two teachers recalled the day, their eyes welled up with tears.

> *"We did not know about it. They just cheered and clapped for us. It was like a cheerleading team for the teachers."*

Having been an assistant dean, dean, and assistant principal at the school for fifteen years prior to taking over, the current principal had a deep understanding of the school's culture. Interestingly, the district rarely promotes administrators internally, typically looking for experienced administrators from other districts. The assistant principal for curriculum and instruction was also a teacher and department chair for seven years at the school prior to her current role. Because of the relationships they established over the years in different roles, nearly every teacher interviewed reported a high degree of relational trust. Six different teachers described the administrative teams' concern for work-life balance. One teacher responded this way:

> I feel like the administration is always concerned about my family—trying to ensure that family work-life balance is there. They are the first people to tell me to not come back the next day if I am sick. This trickles down. As a department chair, I cover teachers' eighth-period classes if they have a sick child at home.

A highly accomplished government teacher with over twenty years of experience explained the vision for teacher leadership development at the school.

> Support, equip, encourage. We receive an incredible amount of support. This is my fourteenth year here, and this is my third and final school. They will have to drag me out of here. As teachers, we see a lot of administrators come and go. This is by far the best group of administrators I have ever worked with. For example, I am a teacher who gets pulled in a lot of directions. The first year that [the principal] was in his office, he yelled my name. I ducked my head and tried to get away. I was always asked to do more things. He yelled, "I know you heard me." I said, "Uh oh." He told me, "You are doing a lot of stuff. What can I do for you? How can I help you?" Whenever I come in with an idea, he tries to support it. I am exhausted and energized by that kind of an environment. I am exhausted, but not drained. My tank is full.

"The 90 Percent Doing a Great Job"

Similar to the rural and urban high schools, the suburban administrators had an open-door policy and much of their communication was face to face. However, the administrative team uses Twitter to highlight the good work that is occurring in classrooms, athletics, clubs, and performing arts. Multiple teachers cited this public support as beneficial. Several teachers also reported going public with their practice because of this. One teacher said, "I also share everything I do on Twitter. I know [the principal] checks that a lot."

A PLC leader and tennis coach described the administrative support in some detail.

> I coach tennis as well. We are certainly not one of the most attended athletic events. The previous principal was not as visible. [The current principal] came to one of the first matches. He is such a positive member of the school community. I don't know how he does what he does with all that he is tweeting out. One of the first things he said at a department chairs meeting—"Our goal for leadership is that we are spreading vision and culture. Every profession and environment is going to have some gripers. As a leadership team, we are going to focus on the 90 percent who are doing a great job. We are going to build their leadership skills." With the department chair at my previous school, the squeaky wheel got the attention. By taking this new leadership approach, you are going to have more of an impact on making good teachers better. We are becoming more transparent and supportive, and It is a healthy transition.

Administrators also knew what was going on in classrooms. They wanted to be in classes more frequently, but when teachers were asked on a scale of 0 to 10 how much administrators knew about what was happening in their classrooms, the average response was 6.7. This was significantly higher than in either the rural or urban high school.

The School Versus "They"

While most of the administrative team believes that they have latitude to support leadership development at their own school, some teachers do not believe there is the same support from the district. One teacher shared,

> This is a top-down district. We even joke now, who is the "they?" We don't even know who "they" are. The district office staff starts to become faceless. The district office becomes the "they." That plays in the favor of our school administration because they are being forced to do stuff as well.

Teachers see freezes on professional learning budgets, required common assessments, and other standardized procedures as emanating from the district office, not their school administrators. One department chair summed up the difference in support. "The practical support comes from the building level. The district is more into what is compliant with state requirements." However, both teachers and administrators describe the way teacher teams develop their own curriculum and that the district does not dictate this. Regardless of the reality of district support for leadership development, the perception of teachers in the building is that they can trust their school administration to be a buffer between them and any externality, including the district.

In three separate interviews, the principal and two of the assistant principals at the suburban high school described the vision their school has for leadership development for the school. The principal described it as "constant growth." The constant growth happens when "we work in teams to try to solve learning problems. Teachers are constantly asking questions. We have to model what we want from students. If we want students to take risks, then as adults we have to model that. It is OK to not get it right the first time." One assistant principal described the vision this way:

> It is something that has developed over time. [The principal] has probably articulated it more than anyone else. It is OK to take chances even if you sometimes fail. It is about learning and growing together. He is always saying, "No one is smarter than everyone in the room."

Another assistant principal described the same vision in slightly different terms. "How can we have teachers lead other teachers? Based on research and support, this is how my students learn; therefore, how can those ideas be shared with other teachers?"

CAPACITY

Teachers leading teachers requires time and capacity. Both teachers and administrators saw some leaders as "stretched thin," although a number of newer teachers were stepping into

5.2 WHAT CAN WE DO RIGHT NOW?

What percentage of administrators and teachers at your school are doing good work? (circle one)

<10%   20%   30%   40%   50%   60%   70%   80%   90%   100%

Does your estimation match others on your team? If not, why are they different?

How are you focusing on, supporting, and celebrating their work?

Who is the "they" at your school? (circle all that apply)

- District administrators
- Students
- Parents
- Community members
- School board
- State policymakers
- Federal policymakers

What development opportunities, if any, are needed to bridge the gap between your school and the "they"?

- Which ones can you make happen?
- How?

leadership roles. Sometimes the passions that cause people to step into leadership can be a challenge. An administrator said, "Part of it is just the exhaustion of certain people. Balance is a challenge. For some of our staff, how they balance their desire to

grow something, a club, or any initiative, with their family life."
A department chair described her goals. "Part of our job is to make
teachers' lives easier—I do not want to ask them to take on more."

Another department chair who had twelve years of experience at other schools believed that there were plenty of opportunities to lead. "At every school I have been at, there is a smaller group
of teachers taking on leadership roles. There is a core group that
does a disproportionate amount of the work. If someone wants
to present or bring something new, I think they have the opportunity." Even with this optimistic view, an administrator still believed
that there were "some people waiting to have an opportunity."

Almost half of the administrators and teachers interviewed
cited the capacity for internal development of expertise through
teacher leadership. One instructional technology coach explained
the importance of feedback in the development of leadership
capacity.

> We use the people who are proven. It is just that when you
> do your job well, others keep asking you to do your job bet-
> ter. We need feedback on how we are doing. We are not
> good at talking about how to improve. You don't get the
> feedback of what was good and what wasn't. I am very
> reflective, but I do not get a lot of feedback. There is not a
> lot of gratification or thanks.

While others echoed this desire for more feedback, some of
this feedback and capacity development is occurring through
in-house institute days. Because of a freeze on money for professional learning, teachers in the building are leading workshops
on practices that worked in their classrooms. A physical education teacher said, "We definitely learn a lot from each other on
those days." Other teachers cited PLCs as "a great step forward
because we began to build leadership within our courses and
departments." The institute days and PLCs are becoming primary
vehicles for leadership development and school improvement.

CONDITIONS AND RESOURCES

Several teachers shared another of the principal's leadership one-
liners that encapsulates the culture of the school: "If you can do

these two things, care and try, we are going to be OK." Many of the teachers went on to describe that the school was about relationships. "Relationships, relationships, relationships. There is general agreement that we are all here to make kids' lives better. We don't all agree on how to do that, but I know if I make good choices then I am OK." This ethos permeated the interviews, classrooms, and hallways.

> *"If you can do these two things, care and try, we are going to be OK."*

Trust and Communication

A social studies teacher who spent seven years at another high school in the district and is now in her second year at this school described the school climate in some detail.

> The atmosphere in the school is very positive. Our kids respect us and that helps us take leadership. Our colleagues respect each other. I don't know how that happens. Our departments are not silo'd—separated from each other. This is not a cliquey place. Everybody says, "Hi" to everybody. I am in a different department's hallway and everybody is very welcoming. Our principal can predict how we are going to feel before we tell him. Administration does not make us compete with each other. We ask, "What can we do to help each other?"

Another teacher described the level of trust in the building. "People are not threatened by innovation. There is a lot of trust. I led a conference of fifty teachers from across the state. After it was over, three administrators contacted me to see if the teachers showed up. That would not happen here." This trust was tested by a new district initiative for more administrative walkthroughs in classrooms. A department chair described how she met this challenge. "I do some of those friendly walkthroughs. The form does not look friendly. I leave chocolate on the teacher's desk with the form. There is a general distrust of the district and general trust of our administration."

These descriptions sounded almost too good to be true, but it was a common refrain from almost every educator. This level of collective leadership does not come without some challenges, however. A math teacher described her perspective. "Teachers have a lot of empowerment. We just sometimes pull in different directions. Once you give that much freedom, education is about a lot of egos, and it becomes hard to always pull in one direction." From several teachers' perspectives, teachers were not involved in certain types of district decisions. "There is a poster in the front hall that describes what the building could look like if a referendum passes. No teachers involved here were involved in that design. Technology is also top-down."

Other teachers observed a generational divide. A department chair explained the challenge. "I am going to divide it into veteran teachers and newer teachers. It is hard for veteran teachers to be much more directed. Half of the teachers in our department are young, enthusiastic teachers who will do whatever you ask them to do. I am right in the middle."

However, in some departments, collaboration is expected. A science department chair explained how shared lab set ups (they share labs to maximize space) and common lessons created these expectations. "In my department, they are so collaborative—there is almost expectation that it would be shared. Why wouldn't you share this with the group? We don't have any lone wolves."

While there were not "lone wolves," PLCs described their autonomy.

> This is one of the strengths of our schools. We will say this is where we are going to be, but each PLC is going to take a different path. I can talk to my PLC about what is working for us. We definitely know what is expected of us, but I am able to determine how to do this. That gives us a lot more wiggle room and acceptance of the process.

The PLC leader contrasted this with her perceived direction of the district. "It seems like our district is moving in the direction of doing everything the same way and the same day."

Part of the foundation of this school culture is communication. Teachers cited face-to-face conversations in PLCs, with department chairs, and administrators. Additionally, there was communication via Twitter and a weekly email referred to as the "Billboard." One teacher described the weekly Billboard. "It is sometimes teacher- or student-focused highlighting something phenomenal that students or teachers are doing and then lists what we need to know for the coming week." The teacher reported that this was in keeping with the style of the principal and was part of the reason he was so well received. "He is very to the point. He always uses that more in an encouraging way. I think sometimes teachers like cynicism, but when someone is actually surprisingly likable, they love him as a principal."

Stretching Resources

Much of this work is done without additional resources. PLC leaders do not receive any compensation for their work. Over forty teachers sponsor student clubs without stipends. This speaks to the level of commitment teachers have to what they are doing, but sustainability can become an issue.

As in other schools, lack of time was mentioned by over half of those interviewed as an obstacle to leadership. Some of the PLCs had a common lunch period where they could work together, but sometimes the tasks required more time than was available. A math teacher described this challenge. "We are on our fourth year of rewriting curriculum because the progression from the district to accommodate Common Core [State Standards] has morphed four times."

5.3 WHAT CAN WE DO RIGHT NOW?

Think about the internal capacity of your school. What does your school need to do to leverage this capacity?

What resources are available to take advantage of the internal expertise of your school?

What conditions are conducive to developing more internal capacity?

WORK DESIGN

At this school, more than at either the rural or urban high school, work was designed for collaboration and leadership development. The principal's description of the way decisions are made at the school indicated the emphasis on the work determining the work design.

> It starts with teachers. What do our best teachers think about this thing? Let's say it is change in practice on our [the administration] level. Take the faculty meeting as an example. I talked to a couple of our best teachers first, then chairs, and then APs. We decided to move the meeting out of the auditorium to the cafeteria. We used to have faculty meetings in the auditorium—it was sit and get. Now, it is in the cafeteria—a large portion of the meeting is teachers talking to teachers. We also have teachers describe what they are doing to other teachers.... Everything we do falls in line with the vision of school as a place to inspire students to continue learning beyond high school. To do that, we have to keep learning and changing.

Several examples illustrate the design of the work.

- Over the previous two years, department chairs had their teaching loads reduced from three teaching periods to two in order to increase their availability to serve their departments.
- All department chairs and administrators meet weekly during the school day. These are highly efficient meetings that end with a recap of what leaders will share from the meeting.
- A Building Leadership Team composed of twelve elected teachers and three administrators meet monthly to discuss other building-related issues.
- The leadership teams are supporting co-teaching efforts of classroom teachers, teachers of English learners (ELs), and special education teachers. Successful co-teaching teams are sharing their ideas with other teams.
- In addition to the biweekly late starts for PLCs, most PLCs share a common lunch period to also connect.

- While both teachers and administrators express the need for more development opportunities, PLC leaders have several lunch trainings per semester to develop their facilitation skills. The district is also working on a change to their compensation structure that will provide a stipend for PLC leadership.

Two particular examples that warrant further examination are PLCs and hybrid roles.

PLCs

According to nearly everyone interviewed, the primary vehicles for school improvement are the PLCs. The PLC leaders facilitate team meetings every other week. Their primary focus over the past three years is creating formative and summative assessments. When asked about outcomes of PLCs, the principal said, "PLCs do not have an endpoint. Teams are on the wheel and just keep improving based on three questions." The three questions are:

- What do we want students to know and be able to do?
- How do we know what they know and are able to do?
- What do we do with students who already know or don't know?

An accomplished special education teacher described the benefit of PLCs.

It is a developing vision. What we have now is freedom. When we started PLCs, leadership really started to change. We no longer waited for the administrators to give us initiatives. The PLCs started doing this. When we started functioning well, we started doing the work that determined the initiatives.

Hybrid Roles

This school is experimenting with a variety of roles for accomplished teachers. For almost every position, administrators and teachers identified internal candidates for these roles. Department chairs are an important part of most of the leadership work that is occurring. They are functioning as both teachers and administrators. Still teaching two periods a day, but also conducting evaluations, doing walkthroughs of classrooms, and making hiring and budgetary decisions. One chair described his biggest challenge in this role.

> I am a quasi-administrator. It took me a year of being a little uncomfortable to overcome that. I am a peer running a department. I think the teachers at our school appreciate that department chairs are teachers. I think that creates a very strong culture because we are doing exactly what they are doing.

Another department chair described her work.

> At least once a week, I am covering a class. We can't pay for subs and students are using my lunch. If you walk around during lunchtime, you will be surprised by how many teachers are talking to students or working at desks. I get emails all the time asking for suggestions. I am walking to the bathroom and I get a teacher asking me how to debrief about interventionists and isolationists? Here we are going to the bathroom and rewriting her lesson plan.

This mix of teaching and administration is challenging, but every department chair I interviewed believes that the combination of roles is essential.

In addition to department chairs, the school created unique teacher roles. One such role is a full-time student activities director who is still paid as a teacher. She considers herself a teacher and she describes numerous teaching and co-teaching activities throughout the day where she connects with students, but she does not oversee any departments or curriculum. "I am not a dean, not an AP, my sole focus is performing arts and activities, not evaluation." In essence, she oversees activities that do not fall under the auspices of the athletic director. Prior to taking over this role, she taught English because she thought "English was the best way to get to know kids." In addition to teaching advanced and remedial English, she coaches a sport, coaches the dance team, works on school musicals, and sponsors the student council. In her words, "student activities are the center of the school. Connecting kids to a school makes them feel that they are a part of a community. In turn, it ensures that they are working harder in the classroom."

Her role as a director allows her to do more of this "connecting" work. She describes her role:

> I handle budgets, transportation, etc. I am also the student liaison. My office is structured so that students can come and go. That is why my office is not in the main office. Anything students want to do to volunteer, they come here. I am also working with a team working on a freshman curriculum for next year. Anything that relates to student leadership, I am on. My days are split between students and sponsors. I meet every morning with the athletic director to coordinate with sports. I think this is very unique to our school. I think in a lot of schools, athletics and activities kind of battle with each other. The athletic director and I work very closely together. We schedule buses together. We have started to streamline— her secretary and my secretary are both in the athletic department and work together. We follow the same rules. I take care of the fundraising for everything, and he does transportation.

Both the hybrid roles and the design of arrangements like this one are deliberate attempts to structure positions around the needed leadership work. The type of flexibility described by the leaders indicates the challenges for this work, but also the opportunity for leadership development when schools are thoughtful about their design.

DEVELOPMENT ACTIVITIES AND EXPERIENCES

Development activities and experiences are closely related to work design at this school. Co-teaching, the work of PLCs, and walk-throughs are three examples of development opportunities.

What role do PLCs play for leadership development at your school?

- If you do not have PLCs, what other vehicles do you have for collective leadership development?

What role do teachers and administrators in hybrid positions play for leadership development at your school?

- If you do not have teachers and administrators in hybrid roles, design three ideal hybrid roles that could develop the leadership your school most needs.

Co-teaching as Leadership Development

Some of the co-teaching at the school is formal and some is informal. Formally, two-teacher teams (e.g., one English teacher and one EL teacher) work together to develop, execute, and assess lessons. School leaders are seeing improved test scores and results for students in these classes. The principal explained, "It has been proven over and over again that this helps students." Several teacher teams have presented their work to other teams at the school. In addition to presenting their work, other teachers reported that they have observed their classrooms to get ideas for their own improvement. An assistant principal describes the work teams are doing in general, and one team in particular.

We are using in-house and external models of co-teaching. Some of our teachers picked up those models quickly. This past institute day, two of our younger teachers led a workshop for teachers across the region on co-teaching. They had a lot of teachers finding them throughout the day.

I talked to them about how they need to take this show on the road. They are both fourth-year teachers and are probably our strongest co-teaching pair in the school. They felt good knowing how much ahead of the curve they were.

Informally, co-teaching is also occurring. One social studies PLC leader shared, "Not only do we walk in and observe, we talk to each other and get involved in the class. We walk in to get something, and then suddenly we are co-teaching with each other. As for it being structured, the opportunity is provided. As PLC leaders, we know that we are moving in the direction of more formal co-teaching opportunities, and that is exciting."

PLCs as Leadership Development

PLCs are hardly unique to this school and have in fact become quite ubiquitous. However, PLCs can take many different forms and serve either as catalysts or impediments for improvement. In the case of the urban high school studied in the previous chapter, several teams were making progress and appreciated the time to collaborate, while others were not progressing. However, far more teams at this school saw the benefit of PLCs. More importantly, the thirty-five facilitators were developed for leadership that was perceived as vital to school improvement. One English PLC leader shared how development was occurring.

> We hold PLC leader meetings a few times a semester, and administration provides lunch. People vent and share things that are working—those ideas really help. PLC leaders are supported in every department, but each one is a little different. For example, the difference between math and English is interesting. English is a little jealous of how black and white assessment is in math. Part of my job is to explain how hard it is to do this in English. Administration supports us in trying to figure things out. I am going to [a high school in a nearby district] to see how their English department is doing their PLCs because they think they have figured this out.

Each department has adapted the PLC department for their own needs, but there are similar themes across the school. A science PLC leader described his approach to their collaboration:

I think our PLC process is designed to do a lot of that collaboration. The teachers here have bought in. Like [the principal] always says, "There is no one in the room smarter than the whole room." I think everyone takes on a leadership role in some respect. We have kept the same PLC leaders for all three years that I have been here, but I think we are going to keep building on having different people rotate leadership. I think that our instructional leadership really builds from the strengths of each team member. Along with that, we have a lot of workshops here that are run by teachers. Teachers are showing how they have integrated new technology or a new strategy. They are leading by example.

In this science PLC, there was no separation between novice and veteran teachers as the work dictated who should lead. In other departments, collaboration was viewed as being a bit different depending on career stage. Four different PLC leaders shared that there was a difference in desire for collaboration, and therefore appreciation of PLCs divided somewhat along generational lines. An English teacher described the benefit of frequent, informal opportunities for collaboration.

The newer teachers are constantly collaborating. The PLC lunches have created a really wonderful collaborative atmosphere. Those lunches have been helpful—most of the PLCs have it. Sometimes more veteran teachers want to stick with what has worked for them, but these informal opportunities for collaboration are helping them to see opportunities for improvement.

With rotating PLC leadership positions that could eventually be compensated, there are strong development opportunities for a wide range of teachers. Along with walkthroughs, PLCs will remain a key component of instructional leadership development.

Walkthroughs as Leadership Development

Another example of work design that was changing at the school was walkthroughs. Both co-teaching and walkthroughs make teaching practice public. Administrative walkthroughs in classrooms have been common for some time in schools. However, leaders at this school were moving to make this common practice for all teachers to conduct walkthroughs as a means of school improvement. At the time of this study, department chairs were conducting walkthroughs as well as administrators. By the following year, teachers were expected to be doing these walkthroughs as well. At the School Improvement Plan (SIP) meeting, administrators and department chairs were discussing what needed to happen next to allow more walkthroughs by teachers:

> We are moving through where we are with the walkthrough guides so that teachers are seeing teaching and giving feedback. When that becomes more of the culture, teachers will take that in. We are trying to communicate that this is how it should be—about getting feedback for improvement and doing that together. We are not doing this for evaluation or for getting people in trouble.

While teachers are not getting to see each other teach as often as they would like, an assistant principal shared her experience as a department chair.

> It [teacher walkthrough] happens a lot more often than it used to occur. As a department chair, I required teachers to observe each other twice a year and as chair, I would cover. Now, we are pushing them to study other departments. We also are pushing teachers to observe co-teaching. We are doing friendly walkthroughs. We hope all teachers will participate in these walkthroughs next year.

Another assistant principal cited the fact that any leadership development that occurs has to be viewed positively. "One thing I think is important, there has to be a way that it feels like an opportunity, not a burden. Teachers have to want to take on some of the tasks and decisions. It is about sharing the vision and disseminating the work. The dirty work should fall on us." To that end, even the walkthrough form was designed through teachers and administrator collaboration. Teachers did not want electronic forms that required observers to be on their computers or tablets in the classroom. Therefore, they are hard copy forms (see Figure 5.1).

Figure 5.1   Walkthrough Form

Teacher: _____   Date: _____   Course: _____

Arrival: _____ AM/PM   Departure Time: _____ AM/PM

Circle one: *First 10 min.*   *Middle of class*   *Last 10 min.*

Focus on Learning
- ❏   Clear objectives/learning targets are posted or stated.
- ❏   Activities in class match/support the stated objective/target.
- ❏   Distraction-free learning environment.
- ❏   Enthusiasm for learning/subject matter apparent from students.
- ❏   Enthusiasm for learning/subject matter apparent from teacher(s).
- ❏   Effective transitions between activities.
- ❏   Evidence of respectful & positive student/teacher relationships.

> Descriptive Feedback:

Student Engagement (FIT: Collaboration & Creation)
- ❏   Students are involved in an activity directly reflecting the posted or stated learning target.
- ❏   Students are actively participating.
- ❏   Students working collaboratively & purposefully in defined groups.
- ❏   Discussion includes higher level questions posed by students.
- ❏   Discussion includes higher level questions posed by teacher(s).
- ❏   Student work reflects development or mastery of posted or stated learning target.

> Descriptive Feedback:

Assessment (FIT: Standards Mastery)
- ❏   Evidence is gathered using a formative assessment.
- ❏   Assessment clearly reflected posted or stated learning target.
- ❏   Instruction is adjusted based on formative assessment evidence.
- ❏   Evidence is gathered using a summative assessment.
- ❏   Descriptive feedback is provided to students.
- ❏   Formative or summative assessment is aligned to a scoring guide or rubric.

> Descriptive Feedback:

It was great to see...

> Descriptive Feedback:

Visitor: _____

5.5 WHAT CAN WE DO RIGHT NOW?

On a scale of 1 to 10, how much co-teaching is occurring at your school?

1 = "None. No one ever leaves their own cell, I mean classroom."

10 = "Constant. Everything is co-taught."

| 1 | 2 | 3 | 4 | 5 | 6 | 7 | 8 | 9 | 10 |

How comfortable are you personally with co-teaching?

How can co-teaching become beneficial as a form of leadership development at your school?

On a scale of 1 to 10, how comfortable are you with walkthroughs by administrators?

1 = "I break out in a cold sweat and see no value in them."

10 = "I love feedback from administrators. I wish they came to my classes daily."

| 1 | 2 | 3 | 4 | 5 | 6 | 7 | 8 | 9 | 10 |

On a scale of 1 to 10, how comfortable are you with walkthroughs by other teachers?

1 = "I break out in a cold sweat and see no value in them."

10 = "I love feedback from teachers. I wish they came to my classes daily."

| 1 | 2 | 3 | 4 | 5 | 6 | 7 | 8 | 9 | 10 |

Is there a difference between these last two scales? Why or why not?

How can walkthroughs become beneficial as a form of leadership development at your school?

INCREASED CAPACITY AND IMPROVED PRACTICE

Increased capacity occurs at the individual and collective level. A contributing factor to the increased leadership capacity seems dependent on the leader's view of the nature of the work or the leader doing the work. Teachers and administrators cited curriculum design, assessment development, and changes in school culture as evidence of improvement. They also cited individual growth.

Leadership: Person or Work?

I asked almost every person I interviewed throughout this study if leadership was more about the person or the work. The responses marked an interesting divide between educators in this school who believed leadership was more about the leader, and those who thought it was about the work. Those educators who believed leadership was more about the person were more likely to believe that someone else needed to identify them as leaders. Those who thought it was about the work were more likely to take on the leadership work and become *de facto* leaders.

One PLC leader's uncertainty over whether or not she was a teacher leader was instructive as she looked for external validation of her status. "I had to ask you if I was the teacher leader. I am lumped with all these other teachers as a PLC leader. No one ever looks at me and says, 'You are a leader.' I wish there was a little more effort to single people out and say, 'Hey, you are really good at this.' They [the administrators] are inconsistent about this." She reiterated, "I had to ask you if I was a leader."

She was concerned about someone else labeling her as a leader. This was concerning as an aspect of school culture and certainly did not define leadership as a set of functions that serve common goals. However, this sentiment was rare. In contrast, an assistant principal saw leadership capacity differently. Teachers were already leading in remarkable ways. The work required to improve the school demanded an endless amount and various types of leadership. She said,

> I am eternally optimistic. I believe the capacity is absolutely infinite. We [administrators] do not want to be in

the way of that. We have done some work with our PLC leaders, but we know more work needs to be done there. Some are comfortable with curricular leadership, but some are not at all comfortable with personnel leadership— for example, some don't want to address teachers who come late.

Areas of Growth

The principal saw PLCs making major changes to curriculum and assessment. These changes were coming from the teams themselves, not through administrative mandates.

> We are leveraging leadership through the PLC process. We have teachers within teams that do a great job. Even when teams have a framework to work through, there is a tremendous amount of freedom for teachers to do their work. Our district did not go out and buy curriculum and standards. Teachers created everything. At a meeting a couple of months ago, I put up some goals we needed to figure out in the next two years—redo's and retakes. Departments don't have to do redo's and retakes. They just have to come to a consensus on what they will do as a team. They can choose to do the redo's and retakes their own way.

This sounds like evidence of increased leadership capacity from the perspective of the principal, but how did teachers feel? Department chairs explained their perspectives.

> The biggest evidence I have is how collaborative our PLC groups are. I would say that our willingness to try new things is evidence. Take retakes, for example. We have teachers that have kind of kick-started that. There is a lot of informal leadership that way. Our physics PLC has taken on the flipped classroom—everyone is using the same format and explaining it to kids. This could be an earth-shattering change, but I have received almost no complaints from parents. Our work is more about the group. It is not about just one person.

Other department chairs saw evidence of impact in other ways. They cited impact through in-house professional learning on institute days and faculty meetings.

> A lot of the stuff that teachers have presented has spread through the school and is present in the classroom. For example, some teachers gave a presentation on Google Classroom, and now a large number of teachers have used it or tried it. A lot of that stuff that teacher leaders have done has become a part of our team. The professional learning feels worthwhile and relevant.

Finally, the school culture is changing. One assistant principal shared, "People now realize that they do not have to get everything right the first time. We are learners." The level of trust and collaboration identified in the 5Essentials survey is more evidence that leadership is having an impact. Is the leadership development responsible for the high level of trust or is the high level of trust responsible for the leadership development? Does it really matter? Administrators and teachers believe both are valuable and mutually reinforcing.

5.6 WHAT CAN WE DO RIGHT NOW?

On a scale of 1 to 10, how would you rate the effect of your school's leadership development efforts on relational trust?

1 = "Leadership development efforts have built a climate reminiscent of the Cold War."

10 = "Leadership development efforts have built a climate of mutual respect, understanding, and deep trust."

| 1 | 2 | 3 | 4 | 5 | 6 | 7 | 8 | 9 | 10 |

Are administrators' and teachers' ratings similar? Are they different?

Based on your results, what needs to happen next in your leadership development efforts?

STUDENT OUTCOMES

At a school where college completion is expected, test scores are high, and graduation rates are high, evidence of improved outcomes can be challenging to find. However, there are signs that leadership development is impacting students.

- Over 70 percent of students are involved in some type of extracurricular activity. There are sixty-seven student clubs ranging from a video game club that raises money for charity to a Future Health Care Professionals Club. There are nineteen performing arts programs and twenty-five sports activities. According to the Student Activities Coordinator, "Anytime a kid wants to start a club, we find a way to make it happen."
- Students' perspectives are being broadened by life-changing experiences. I was sitting in the office waiting to conduct another interview when a teacher started talking to a student with a large duffle bag. The students were about to head to the airport for their music trip to China. The teacher asked, "Are you excited?" The student replied, "I am excited, but a little nervous. I have never been on a plane or been out of the country." Because of the leadership of several music educators, this student who had never been on a plane was on her way to China.
- Finally, a special education teacher described the change in the school culture over the past several years—a change that has affected both teachers and students. "I think [the school] is becoming a school that takes risks because we know we have leaders who want to improve."

FEEDBACK LOOPS

If improvement is desired, feedback is essential. The larger the school, the more intentional leaders have to be about collecting feedback. One good example of feedback changing what school leaders are doing is related to their data management system. In a department chairs meeting, they described the "brief, but storied history" of their data management system:

It is just bad. We need to move on, it doesn't work. We can choose some other system that other districts are using and know that they are going to work. We are going to have to go in front of the school board and say, "We need something different," after we went in front of the board and said we need this.

Obviously, this is difficult for leadership, but they described the need for this because of feedback. One department chair elaborated, "There is a definite sense that things we are going to change are going to come from the ground up. The ideas are going to come from the teachers. It has to come from the expertise of a dedicated group of teachers that will move outward."

This works both for positive change and for pushing back on things that do not work, according to another department chair. "When teachers see something as valuable, they work very well collaboratively. If you give them something that is trivial or not related to student success, then they become a very different group to work with. That is how it should be."

THE BLUEPRINT

Whether I returned in the role of a teacher or student, I wanted to return to high school—not just any high school, but this high school. I honestly did not know that high schools like this really existed. From the monthly thirty-minute teacher-led staff meetings; to PLCs where teachers work together to make their lives easier, and teaching more effective; to students who open doors for strangers on cold, dreary mornings; there were so many things that spoke to a different kind of culture. The cause *and* the evidence of this difference can be found in the way teachers, administrators, and teachers speak about each other. They all describe the respect they have for each other's work, and particularly for the work they do together. Certainly, there are some teachers at the school who feel that there are top-down mandates, or feel that some teachers have more influence than others. I am sure that others are unhappy. However, those in leadership— teachers, administrators, and students—choose to focus on the work and those doing the work. This creates a self-perpetuating cycle of improvement. The leadership work leads to more work that leads to more results that shape the school. Those doing the work are the *de facto* leaders, and they are proud of the work they are doing.

How the district and school will work together to develop more structures, hybrid positions, and resources to support the needs of leadership development remains to be seen. However, the relational trust, culture, and work seem oriented toward growth.

Chapter Review: What Matters Most for Schools (and in This Chapter)?

- ❖ A monthly thirty-minute high school staff meeting that is teacher-led exists.

- ❖ Sometimes promoting from within is essential for building trust and developing leadership.

- ❖ Focus on the 90 percent.

- ❖ Avoid "they."

- ❖ Leaders who believe leadership is more about the work than the person seem to have greater capacity.

- ❖ "If you can do these two things, care and try, we are going to be OK."

- ❖ Department chairs can function as effective hybrid teacher leaders if the right people are in those positions. When aligned with PLCs, they build a strong culture of continuous improvement.

- ❖ Co-teaching and walkthroughs are effective vehicles for leadership development and taking teaching public.

- ❖ Leadership development broadens students' experiences.

- ❖ Sometimes leadership development means learning to say when things are not working.

Action Steps

Depending on the level of trust in your school, you will have more or fewer opportunities to develop the kind of leadership you need. One of the best ways to build that trust is through collective leadership work. What are some steps you can take to develop both leadership and trust?

What could you do with:

- Staff meetings?
- Focusing on the 90 percent?
- Avoiding "they"?
- PLCs?
- Co-teaching?
- Walkthroughs?
- Hybrid roles?
- Expanded opportunities for students?
- Identifying things that are not working?

For Administrators:

1. Co-plan meetings and development opportunities with teachers.
2. Identify three ways to reduce the length of meetings. Use time limits.
- What can be communicated through emails?
- What decisions have to be made?
- What discussions are needed?

(Continued)

(Continued)

For Teachers:

3. Identify three ways that you can be more engaged in staff, team, or PLC meetings by identifying ways you can contribute, anticipating what you can gain, and reflecting on what you have learned.

4. Identify one leadership development opportunity you will pursue, and one thing you will say "no" to.

For Administrators and Teachers:

5. Take five minutes to sit down with a teacher or administrator to ask three questions:

- What creates the most stress in your work?

- What are you most excited about in your work?

- How could I better support you?

CHAPTER 6

Ideal Leaders, Not Solo Superheroes

"Performance is the currency of autonomy."

The reality is that I was able to do whatever I wanted to do in my science lab, because my students demonstrated high value-added scores on state assessments. Value-added scores are derived from students' past performance on state assessments and predict how they should perform in a given year. I was selected to be a Teaching Fellow at the U.S. Department of Education in large part due to my students' value-added scores. I worked with many great colleagues and was connected to some excellent organizations, such as the Center for Teaching Quality and the National Institute for Excellence in Teaching. My professional world expanded.

Unfortunately, that growing professional sphere did not include the rest of my school. The autonomy I had in my classroom allowed me to close my door and isolate myself. My experiences through the fellowship opened doors for me, but at the same time closed doors for me at my school. I was developed for work that did not translate to the limited opportunities in my school and district. In some ways, my performance isolated me from great colleagues at my school.

Eight years later, on a few hot, sticky summer days in North Carolina, I began to see what could happen when autonomy is linked to performance. The Center for Teaching Quality (CTQ) convened fifteen identified teacher leaders for a retreat. In a researcher's dream role, I was able to interview all fifteen leaders and then conduct a focus group with them to better understand how they had developed as leaders. Not only was I able to interview each of them, I was also able to conduct follow-up interviews every three months for a year after the retreat to register their continued development.

I hesitate to share too much about these teachers, because what they are doing is not about them. They would be the first to tell you this. I also do not want to reinforce the teacher hero mythology. But you need a glimpse of the work that they are doing with others.

By way of brief introduction, these were some of the best elementary, middle, and high school teachers in the country. They are doing cutting-edge work with visual note-taking (using graphics to capture ideas), social justice, and problem-based learning, and their voices extend well beyond the classroom to outlets like *The Atlantic* magazine. Most of them are National Board Certified Teachers (NBCTs), and all of them are recognized as outstanding practitioners. Some are just beginning to be recognized as leaders. Some are just beginning to recognize themselves as leaders. They are accomplished teachers who meet with similarly skilled colleagues, but they are not superheroes. What really brings them together is the notion that they want to do more for their students, and they might be able to do more together.

I had two primary questions I was attempting to answer in my work with them:

1. How have these teachers developed as leaders?

2. How do their experiences compare to what I found at the three high schools and in the literature represented by the model?

In this chapter, I share their experiences to illustrate what the work of ideal leaders looks like.

CATALYTIC ADMINISTRATIVE SUPPORT

Every one of the teacher leaders interviewed cited administrative support as key to their development. When asked, "How much do school administrators know about what is occurring in your classroom (0 = nothing, 10 = everything)?" Their average response was 4. While administrators in the high schools typically rated their knowledge higher than this, this rating was almost identical to the responses of teachers across all three schools. The point is that teachers perceive that administrators know something about what is occurring in their classrooms and that teachers who reported greater administrator knowledge of their classrooms also reported higher levels of administrator support in general.

Another similar finding was the lack of flexible leadership development. Not only was administrative support important, administration was seen as a primary means of increasing influence. Fourteen of the fifteen teachers saw the primary way to lead outside the classroom in their districts was to go into administration. All of the teachers cited a need for more hybrid roles for teachers to work with both teachers and administrators while still

> *All of the teachers cited a need for more hybrid roles for teachers to work with both teachers and administrators while still maintaining teaching responsibilities.*

6.1 WHAT CAN WE DO RIGHT NOW?

On a scale of 1 to 10, how much do administrators know about what is going on in classrooms at your school?

0 = "Nothing"

10 = "Everything"

1	2	3	4	5	6	7	8	9	10

Is there a difference between administrators' and teachers' responses? What does this tell you?

What opportunities are there for more hybrid roles at your school?

What obstacles are there for more hybrid roles at your school?

maintaining teaching responsibilities. Several teacher leaders, like the Denver teacher in a hybrid role whose quote begins the chapter, had already assumed these roles in their districts and found administrative support to be even more essential.

Catalyst

1. *Responsible for supporting the change*
2. *Does not cause the change*
3. *The catalyst is not the focal point; the change is.*

In science, a catalyst is a substance that causes a chemical reaction to occur at a faster rate but is not involved in the reaction. This is an important definition on three levels. First, the catalyst is responsible for supporting a change. Second, the catalyst does not cause the change. Third, the catalyst is not the focal point; the change is.

In education, neither the catalytic administrator nor the teachers are the focus. The work is the focus. What is generated by the work is something new and different. Having served in several hybrid roles, the teacher leader who said, "Performance is the currency of autonomy," described his relationship with one particular catalytic administrator.

> My principal was an assistant principal over my department during my first two years of teaching. He was my mentor teacher. His guidance was incredible. He moved to a middle school and then moved to a high school, so I moved to join him there in a hybrid role. Outside of him, I have worked with principals who trusted me and got out of the way to allow me to do what I needed to do to grow professionally. That has been huge.

Two other teachers reported leaving a school to follow a principal. In the focus group, the teacher leaders expressed a desire for relationship and trust with an administrator. Those who had trust reported that this had grown over time and through working together toward common goals.

Another teacher leader described the difference district administration can make.

> I had district leadership that was not open to new curricular ideas, or any ideas from teachers. That is one of the reasons I switched districts. That was six years ago.

6.2 WHAT CAN WE DO RIGHT NOW?

How can we foster more catalytic teachers and administrators who better understand each other and can then work together?

Who are the catalytic leaders in your building?
How can you do more work with them?

Our current principal and district administration support innovative curriculum ideas. They encourage teachers to get involved in professional learning and district-level work even though there is no official development.

This teacher leader now serves in a hybrid role spending half his time in the classroom and half his time organizing leadership efforts across the district.

CAPACITY

"I never thought of myself as a leader until..." In interview after interview, this was a common refrain from the identified teacher leaders. Most of the teacher leaders described work that changed their perceptions of themselves as leaders. These changes in perception significantly impacted their capacities. Typically, the work preceded their self-identification as leaders.

I had a moment. When I was district Teacher of the Year, I got invited to conversations that I wasn't privy to before that. I got invited to an elevating teaching conference. The three days were about helping us view ourselves as leaders. Obviously before that, I had to do some leadership work, but I had not thought of myself that way. I met [another teacher in the CTQ
(Continued)

(Continued)

network] at the conference, and I did work with her. Because my eyes had been opened in these conversations, I realized I needed to do the work that I was passionate about.

Shortly after the conference, my son and I were driving past our school, and he asked me, "Mommy, is my teacher going to be brown?"

My answer was, "No, but she will be really nice."

But that is when I realized I needed to do something. I went to my superintendent, and said, "I am ready to use my voice to bring more brown teachers to [our district]." I did not know it was going to be me doing it, but it was. I struggled to find other people doing the work, so I reached out to them via Twitter to find people. Recruiting and retaining teachers of color is a much larger part of the national conversation now than it was four years ago.

Identity and Capacity

Teacher leaders described the influence of their identities on their capacity for leadership. One teacher leader shared:

What I lacked when I came in [to teaching] was identity. I did not know how to use who I was to be more effective. The title was important and moving into administration was important. I have really worked on knowing who I am. When I decided to be a really good teacher every day, that is when everything started coming together.

This was a common theme. Being a "good teacher every day" mattered a lot to each of the teacher leaders. More than just credibility, this identity was the starting point from which they derived their mandate to lead.

A veteran teacher leader shared the challenges that came with not being seen as a teacher or leader at her school even though she was having an influence at state and national levels. Teachers were unaware of her practice because of the closed classroom doors, and they were unaware of her leadership beyond their context because her work was outside of their context. This was beginning to change.

> I stay because I care about my students and they are my community. I think my students deserve to have a teacher who went to Stanford University and came from the same impoverished life that they do. To have Latinas go, "She is just like us, and she has traveled. She went to Stanford." I want to be able to be a role model. I want to be there for parents. I am starting to get some questions about how I do things.

Potential Capacity

When teachers who identified themselves as leaders were asked, "On a scale of one to ten, with one being completely tapped out and ten only scratching the surface of your capacity, how would you rate yourself?" the average response was eight. From any perspective, these teachers were extremely busy within and beyond the classroom, and yet, they felt they had far more to give.

They also believed that other teachers in their buildings had significantly more potential capacity. A lack of awareness of opportunities and fear of vulnerability were keeping other teachers "chained up." One teacher leader in the focus group said, "Hella [a large number of] teachers are at 'one' because they think they are still chained up. They don't know to try anything different. Is it that you are at a 'one', or is that you are not willing to be vulnerable?" Another teacher leader added, "If you think a ceiling is always there, it is. Even in those circumstances where there is a ceiling, we can find other ways to exceed."

> *"If you think a ceiling is always there, it is."*

One teacher leader who was near the limit of his capacity saw that as a positive. "Our district is open to new roles, and I have support from external organizations like CTQ. My capacity is tapped, but in a good way because I am in a hybrid role. I am at a 'two' not because I am constrained, but because I am tapped." One teacher cited the hope that his principal saw in the potential leadership in their building. "My principal is all about it [leadership development]. He knows he is going to be a better principal if he lets his teachers be the experts that they are."

Work and Capacity: "It's About the Work."

When asked, "Is leadership more about the leader or the work?" teachers who had a greater impact on their schools, colleagues, and students viewed leadership as more about the work than the leader (fourteen out of fifteen). One teacher leader explained, "I feel like when it is about the work, the leadership comes naturally as a by-product of it. I cannot think of any teacher leader anywhere who became a teacher leader because they wanted to be. It was because of the work that others identified them as leaders." The most accomplished teacher leaders in the high schools took on work that stirred their passions. The implications of this seem clear. In order to improve development, it seems important to shift teachers' and administrators' mindsets to consider leadership as work rather than a job title, which, in turn, dictates the way teachers' leadership work evolves and the leader's sense of efficacy.

> I just know that I feel very actualized as a teacher. That does take that extra time. I will put in a fifteen-hour day and run a webinar. It does finally feel like I have found what I am really supposed to do. I am excited to be in education when I see a major shift happening. I want to be sure that the shift encompasses all learners. Because of that, my leadership style has changed. I was a lot louder in my leadership. Now, I am enjoying being quiet in my leadership and looking for other leaders to develop. I know what it takes to become a leader and I am looking for others to cultivate. I am more interested in developing [another teacher leader] than I am in myself. I am able to see leadership qualities in students as well. I don't look for the cheerleader and football player anymore. I think there is real power for a disengaged student to have an impact on the student body and to develop their skills.

The teacher leaders who were describing their greatest impact were not focused on themselves. In fact, they were looking for others to step up to improve student outcomes.

6.3 WHAT CAN WE DO RIGHT NOW?

How has your identity as an educator affected your willingness and ability to lead?

Based on who you are as an educator, what development opportunities would you like to take advantage of?

How does thinking about leadership as work affect your willingness to lead?

CONDITIONS THAT PROMOTE COLLECTIVE LEADERSHIP DEVELOPMENT

The more removed teacher leaders were from decision making, the more top-down mandates they were forced to comply with, the more toxicity they described in their contexts. Teachers were more likely to describe their school setting as toxic in districts where administrators did not work to develop leadership in teachers (See Figure 6.1).

When asked, "What is the most important school condition that constrains teacher leadership development?" teachers cited a range of issues familiar in most schools.

- "Traditional school view of what school is and how it runs."
- "Inability to triage—when everything is important then nothing is."
- "A lose/win culture around leadership. External pressures like accountability influence this."
- "Secrets. People use knowledge as a weapon."

In contrast, when asked, "What conditions support leadership development?" teacher answers included:

- "Freedom"
- "Inclusivity for all, not a select few"

Figure 6.1   Top Down Policy and Toxicity

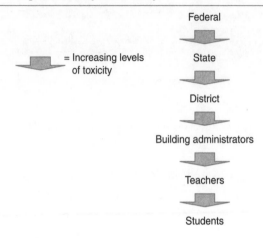

- "Capacity for risk taking"
- "Vision and purpose"
- "Acknowledgement that a teacher is an expert"
- "Collaboration"
- "Trust"
- "Transparency about what you're doing and experiencing"
- "Getting rid of ego!"
- "Flexibility"
- "Shared leadership roles between administrators and teachers"

Escaping the "Crab Bucket"

Dan Duke (2008) compared toxic schools to crab buckets. Crab buckets do not need lids because as soon as one crab gets close to climbing up the side and out, the other crabs pull it back down. He observed this same phenomenon in schools where teachers who are recognized for excellent teaching or who move too far beyond the classroom are sometimes sabotaged by other teachers.

Teacher leaders describe these cultures that are less than con-ducive to development.

Teachers gossip and turn it into a group discussion in the staff room. They are talking and complaining, but who's hearing it? Only people who also take it negatively and don't do anything. Teachers can snipe at each other too. A teacher steps up to work with administration and others say, "Why is she getting that? Why does she get to do that?" It's that they [the sniping teachers] never asked! If you stepped up and asked, then you could also do things.

Some teacher leaders are beginning to see shifts in the "crab bucket" culture. When they are able to propose work that allows others to say "yes" because administrators, teachers, and students can see benefits, they are able to build coalitions. The key is making it easy to say yes. Seven basic principles to achieve this include:

1. Make it about students.

2. Keep costs down or provide ideas for how to fund.

3. Enlist the help of key supporters informally before proceeding formally.

4. Demonstrate small successes, preferably with improved student outcomes.

5. Seek the expertise of others—not buy-in. No one wants to be sold a plan.

6. Emphasize that teachers and administrators are on the same team.

7. Remember, the work is not about you.

Trust and Patience

New ideas and initiatives take time. One teacher leader wanted to remind states and districts when they implemented a new initiative, "It will work, but maybe not by December. They are very quick to abandon all types of projects before they can show results. Results might take more than a school year." For example, a teacher in Iowa cited an initiative to develop teacher leadership in his

> *"One teacher leader wanted to remind states and districts when they implemented a new initiative, 'It will work, but maybe not by December.'"*

state. "Our state government gave millions to districts to create teacher leadership positions. There are some good things going on, and other things have potential, but we do not have student outcome data yet."

Part of that needed patience with initiatives is grounded in trust. If there is trust in the initiative and those people who are implementing it, then patience is more likely. One high school teacher leader said, "Trust is something we all need. Anytime an administrator trusts a teacher to do something then they're likely to carry it out. When I have the trust of my colleagues, I am going to produce a good end product." When that trust only occurs in the classrooms of some teachers, trust erodes. A teacher leader from a charter school said,

> What we do in my school is give more autonomy inside the classroom for good teachers. What we get wrong is that when a teacher does something well like PBL [problem-based learning], we want every other teacher to do that same thing. This takes away autonomy for leadership, and other teachers may not be able to teach like that.

6.4 WHAT CAN WE DO RIGHT NOW?

In order to give administrators a reason to say "yes," you need to be ready to say "yes" and support others, but you also need to frame proposed work as something that benefits everyone—administrators, teachers, and students.

- What is the work that you see as most needed to improve outcomes for students? How can you support or what can you do that works in such a way that is easy for decision makers to say "yes?"

- What financial, human, and community resources does your school have?

- How can those resources create conditions conducive to leadership development (e.g., freedom, inclusivity, trust, risk-taking, and flexibility)?

WORK DESIGN

Because these teacher leaders were in diverse school contexts, the design of their work was not uniform. The teacher leaders who reported the most collective leadership development opportunities were in hybrid roles or had worked closely with administrators on collaborative projects. All of the fifteen teacher leaders described a desire for hybrid roles that allowed them to lead without leaving the classroom; however, most of their districts did not have these types of positions.

DEVELOPMENT ACTIVITIES AND EXPERIENCES

The teacher leaders reported three striking things about leadership development: very little was systematic, there were almost no opportunities for administrators to develop with teacher leaders, and there were disconnects between internal and external development.

Organic Development Opportunities

Formal development experiences for teachers and administrators are rare. However, teacher leaders did cite some growth on the part of school administrators who were becoming more comfortable with some aspects of teacher leadership. "Our principal has started to ask teachers to share new ideas for five to ten minutes in staff meetings." Another teacher leader briefly described informal opportunities for interaction, if not development. "Our principal supports innovative suggestions for curriculum ideas, and encourages teachers to get involved in professional learning and district-level work. There is no official development."

When teachers and administrators collaborated at the school or district level, a deeper appreciation for the work of others made progress toward mutual goals more likely. It also led to a deeper understanding of the other's roles and perspectives. When teachers are working with school or district administrators, they are less likely to believe that they are unfeeling "others" conspiring to make their lives harder.

Internal Versus External Development

Because there are limited development opportunities in districts, teacher leaders are externally developing themselves. This results in more activated teacher leaders. One middle school teacher described an experience working on a team with state legislators and administrators. "In that state-level group, everyone in that group viewed me as an equal. I am thinking 'I am *just* this classroom teacher,' but I was a peer. We were expected to present across the state, and that pushed me out of that shell." This idea of being "just" a teacher is telling and common in the teacher leaders who are just beginning to find their leadership footing. Others cited the need for external validation of their leadership.

> My work with [a state-level organization] helped me understand that I have a voice outside my district and could contact people at the state level. State legislators were writing bills, and I could get them to understand my perspective. The organization put me in front of legislators and business leaders and I got grilled with questions as if I was in a fishbowl. I realized then that I could talk to anybody. Senators, district leaders, and business leaders do not scare me.

This kind of external development can be challenging for schools as well as the developing leader. One teacher shared, "I am definitely cooler outside of my own building than in it."

Other teachers turned to social media for development. "I felt really isolated so I started using Twitter, then for the sake of growth constantly pushing myself to places where I am uncomfortable. I was always activated, but once my eyes were opened, it became something I wanted to make others aware of."

An elementary teacher leader described her epiphany as she became more connected beyond her district. Her district was a nationally recognized district that had received a large philanthropic investment.

> It came as a complete shock to me that there were people outside of the district who knew how to do things. It had been so ingrained in me that we had to do things the "[Name of District] Way." Twitter has broken that down.

My supervisor saw that I was getting things done. After five years of wearing him down, I finally did an unconference [informal exchange of ideas among participants] with media specialists this February. It was successful, and now the district is going to do it again.

Here is one example of a teacher who learned to lead by letting go and allowing his students to lead.

The culture of being a teacher leader in our district meant having a title. When I started teaching there, I was ambitious to a fault. I stepped out of my comfort zone. I am normally very introverted, but I tried to step out of that and become a very loud, ambitious person. Ultimately, it culminated in my principal telling me to "shut up, get back in line, and do my job." That for me was kind of a lynchpin moment. My goal clarity coach, kind of a hybrid teacher leader role in the district, told me, "Use this as an opportunity grow and be better. Just focus on your craft. You are already a good teacher; now is the time to be great." Through that process, I learned that leadership is not title; leadership comes when you are doing what is best for students every day. That was a big thing for me, embracing who I was. It was a shot to my pride, but worth it in the end.

I realized I needed to diversify my teaching practice to improve, so I decided to pursue PBL [Problem Based Learning] through the district. I went through the training and spent six months networking with people in our local school community to identify problems our students could tackle. In the past, I focused on what position I needed to get, but after the PBL, in three months I got more recognition from parents, students, and the community than I had in six years. To me that really validated that leadership can come from doing that work on the front end, taking a step back, and letting the kids find their way. We spent three months doing the project, and during that time I "taught" very little, and the kids did everything. I had so many teachers come

(Continued)

(Continued)

to me and say, "I wish I could let go like that," and that was kind of a big insight for me. My kids live in a food desert in the city. They had no idea where their food came from. We jumped down the rabbit hole of figuring out the source of their food. We brought in farmers, grocers, and chefs. The students had to create recipes based on their research and argue why theirs was the best based on economics, environment, and health. The winner got their recipe put on the menu of a local restaurant for a week. The academic stuff was cool, but the amazing result was the life skills learned.

INCREASED CAPACITY AND IMPROVED PRACTICE

These development opportunities led to various levels of increased capacity for the teacher leaders and their students. The improvement was sometimes described as individual progress, but other teacher leaders reported indicators of broader progress. Sometimes the growth was incremental. Sometimes it was exponential, but the key to improvement was relational influence.

Incremental Improvement

Examples include:

- Teachers reported experiencing increased capacity as a result of reflecting on their practice with others.
- At least one teacher was inspired to earn NBCT certification and thereby work toward ongoing improvement in his own practice.
- Another teacher reported having the confidence to begin working outside of his department (English) by collaborating with a teacher in the Reading department.
- Others cited increased confidence, more partners in collaboration, and increases in the number of opportunities for others to lead.

- As a result of increased capacity and a sense of advocacy, a teacher inspired a school to form a fifteen-person committee to work on equity issues.

Exponential Influence

Examples include:

- One teacher leader increased capacity so much that he was in the process of refining his story for five upcoming speeches.
- Two of the teachers mentioned that they now had thousands of followers on Twitter.

When asked what evidence illustrated his growing impact, one teacher shared:

It depends on the type of evidence you are looking for. I have been asked to lead professional development and training for teachers and school districts across the nation—from Tulsa, Oklahoma, to Florida, to New Orleans, to Fairbanks, Alaska. I have helped our district articulate their equity work around our district leading professional development. I have blogged about it. I was on the Teacher Advisory Council with the Gates Foundation due to all the work we were doing. We got to really push the envelope on a lot of things with them. When I started, equity and culturally responsive education was not on their radar; now they have a whole department devoted to this. That was based on a handful of us on the Teacher Advisory Council saying we need quantitative and qualitative data to tell you why this is important.

Some teachers were also having exponential impact in large districts and at the school level.

The superintendent has been open to teacher involvement with the Gates Foundation, EdCamps [participant-driven professional learning], and CTQ. She is starting to see that teachers can be leaders. We have our first EdCamp next week. She supports this voice project where we secured

$50,000 in funding and will train thirty virtual community organizers. There are new opportunities for teachers to step into roles that did not exist before. We have blended learning happening in our high school, and there are over fifty students who applied to participate.

Much of this influence is spread through the work. In the case above, little thought was given to development of teachers or administrators, but the work itself, done in partnership between educators, resulted in leadership development that supported school goals.

Relational Influence

Relational trust and relationship development are positive drivers of increased capacity. Sometimes the relationship is between one teacher and one administrator. "There is one administrator who listens to me a lot. She has the ability to make decisions, and now she is advocating a lot more for teacher leadership." Another teacher leader described the way these relationships develop:

> What we have seen working well is people having human conversations. They are presenting what they tried or learned with the pros and cons of how it actually played out in the classroom. They are not putting themselves out there as the best teacher or saying, "This went perfectly" to where it is an unattainable thing; but they also aren't trashing it. It is the next step of what I'll do differently next time to make things better. They are keeping it real, but describing the payoff. That is something you don't always get in professional development. We are remembering that if you don't have a relationship with students or colleagues, they are not going to learn from you. We are now talking about critical friends' conversations. How do you help people see what they need to improve? It is part of the norms of our profession and moving away from the attitude, "It is not my kid, and I am not the principal."

The relational influence was obvious in the retreat. Several teacher leaders described how other leaders in the room had mentored them and connected them to new professional resources.

At your school, what are the most influential relationships on your leadership development?

What is one thing you can do to increase your influence on at least one other person?

What is one leadership development opportunity that you could take advantage of to learn with someone else?

For example, two of the teachers connected around a shared passion for visual note-taking when they were only connected virtually through CTQ. As other teachers were learning about visual note-taking at the retreat, they were arranging to Skype the experts in the group into their classrooms. The relational trust that was developed resulted in increased influence and the spread of expertise.

STUDENT OUTCOMES

The improved practice of these teacher leaders is directly impacting student learning.
Examples include:

- Students in Wisconsin and North Carolina are collaborating and improving their note-taking skills. In one school, students are uploading visual notes online so that classmates can see what each class is doing.
- Teachers see examples of improvement in teachers' capacity to advocate for all students, not only students whose race they shared.
- There are also reports of students' increased capacity to advocate for themselves.
- One teacher successfully advocated for de-tracking students in math. The school saw improvements on common math assessments for all students, particularly for students of color.

- A business teacher reported significant academic improvements when the school collectively moved to competency-based curriculum. A competency-based curriculum requires students to provide evidence that they have actually learned.
- An elementary teacher described what her PLC was doing as they had taken steps to make their time more valuable:

> Instead of just going through the motions and completing required protocols, we researched strategies, co-planned the lessons, and even co-taught with an emphasis on metacognition. Our test scores reflected growth, particularly in reading comprehension and in the mathematical shifts—for example, explaining your thinking. That is the physical evidence that proves that this co-teaching, modeling thing works.

- For a high school English teacher, all that was needed was some autonomy and student inspiration:

> Creating the high school literary magazine was a very influential event because the administration wasn't supportive of it or against it, so I got autonomy. Because it was student-led, it really inspired me. We were creative and thought outside of the box. We interviewed fourteen Pulitzer Prize winners and recorded Maya Angelou's last recorded interview on the phone. Because of experiences like this, I saw more engagement from students. They took more ownership of their education.

FEEDBACK LOOPS

Capturing what is working for administrators, teachers, and students is challenging. Whether formal or informal, feedback loops in the development of leadership were not obvious to the teachers. However, they did describe the complexity of their work and the need for feedback loops that might capture and lead to improvement.

As several teacher leaders described, both administrators and teachers faced challenges.

> There is an administrative bureaucracy that has to be carefully navigated. The politics of that can be distracting. One element of that is the need to always make people think they came up with the idea. Other teachers are set in their ways and do not really see the need to collaborate. Teachers are very territorial in their classrooms, which in some ways is a good thing. They are kings and queens of their classrooms, which makes them very comfortable, but they are closed off to being observed by other teachers and collaborating openly and transparently with other teachers. That lack of openness is an obstacle.

Most of the teacher leaders agreed that they had to be savvy about how to present ideas and feedback. Repeatedly, they mentioned the need to share credit and allow others to think an idea was theirs. Most of them found this to be acceptable because it was about "doing what is best for kids."

Another teacher leader voiced frustration with what I call the "Retreat Effect"—everyone gets excited about a shared vision at a retreat, and then nothing changes as a development experience because we return to a reality that was not changed by the retreat. Much of the frustration has to do with a lack of communication, shared experience, and a development of followership (Day, Zaccaro, & Halpin, 2004). Another teacher leader described a lack of understanding of how to move ideas forward.

> There seems to be a disconnect between our ideas and where we are. When we sit here and talk to each other, it all makes sense. I am not sure how to navigate Central Office. How do we connect the people who can help with this? I know I need to be patient, but I am not.

One teacher leader described a solution to this problem, and it involved feedback that spoke the language of her district administrators. "Our deputy superintendent talks about ROI [return on investment]. Figuring out how to quantify what we are doing would help. We have to figure out how to tell our stories to people that have the power to remove barriers."

Two other issues that we spend more time with in Chapter 7 also seem to be at play here. First, sometimes leadership means listening, but saying "no" to ideas. Leaders—teachers and administrators alike—cannot say, "yes" to every idea that is generated in a building or district. Sometimes, they are not good ideas. This leads to a lack of coherence around shared vision and stretches resources to a breaking point. The idea of ROI captures part of this idea. Second, as leaders, we have to make it easy for others to say, "yes." That means providing evidence of positive impact on students, identifying necessary resources, and engaging the right partners for the work. Sometimes that means saying "yes" to others' ideas or building on their work.

6.6 WHAT CAN WE DO RIGHT NOW?

Leadership development in complex environments can be challenging and difficult to quantify. As you read these chapters, you notice how hard it is for leaders to provide quantifiable ROI. There are many reasons for this—the complexity of contexts, the challenge of changing cultures, the various needs of individuals—but the real question is: "What kind of feedback do we need to determine if we are successful and/or adjust course?"

So that is the question for your school and leadership team: "What kind of feedback do we need to determine if we are successful and/or adjust course?"

Do you already have those data?

What else do you need?

How can you collect these data in a fair and efficient manner?

If you are hitting a dead end with your influence, what are you doing to make it easy for others to say "yes" to your ideas? What are you saying "yes" to as well?

SOLO SUPERHEROES NO MORE

As I continue to follow up with these teacher leaders, I hear their triumphs, their frustrations, and the thin line between changing a system and throwing in the towel. They share their experiences every few months in an online focus group via Zoom, an online collaboration tool that creates a Brady Bunch–like screen filled with talking heads. I ask a few questions and then just listen and take notes.

When they are together, they are powerful.

They commiserate, encourage, exhort, and advise.

Most of all, they are present.

Which means they are not alone.

A few of the teacher leaders have this kind of community in their schools and districts—a community that includes teachers and administrators. Many do not. It is my hope that schools, districts, and organizations like CTQ will do even more to bring together teachers, administrators, and even students to do the gritty, real leadership work needed to improve outcomes for all kids. Where trust does not exist, wisdom and skillful facilitation is needed to create space for meaningful conversation. Not everyone has to lead, but everyone has to follow wisely, and we can only lead and follow together.

Chapter Review: What Matters Most for Schools (and in This Chapter)?

❖ Performance should equal autonomy, not isolation.

❖ We need more catalytic administrators—ones who support a change and are not the focal point.

❖ Teachers and administrators working together are more likely to enact meaningful change than teachers working around administrators or administrators flying solo.

❖ A leader's identity impacts his or her capacity for leadership development.

❖ As leadership evolves, the leader becomes invested in developing leadership in others.

❖ Escape the "crab bucket" by making it easy for others to say "yes."

❖ Where there is more trust, there is more patience. Results are more likely to follow if schools and districts stick with an initiative.

❖ Hybrid roles are key to bringing together teachers and administrators in leadership work.

❖ Sometimes external development is necessary to validate internal leadership.

❖ Whether improvement is incremental or exponential, it is always relational.

❖ The art of leadership development: Share the credit.

❖ How much attention are you paying to the development of followership and relational trust?

Action Steps

For Administrators:

1. Identify a leadership development opportunity that can be pursued with teachers.
2. Consider hybrid roles that can allow you to co-teach or step back into the classroom. At minimum, find some time to teach students.
3. Talk to three teachers about their own leadership development to find out what is frustrating and what is promising.

For Teachers:

4. Identify a leadership development opportunity that can be pursued with an administrator.
5. Consider hybrid roles that can allow you to take on a different leadership task. Build on your credibility as an effective teacher.
6. Talk to an administrator about their own leadership development to find out what is frustrating and what is promising.

For Administrators and Teachers:

7. Reexamine the areas you identified that require leadership development. What steps can you take to better develop those areas?

   a. What can you do internally?

   b. Who are possible external partners?

(Continued)

(Continued)

 c. What can you do to informally develop leadership?

 d. What formal steps can you take?

8. Identify teacher leaders or peer leaders in your school or district with whom you can co-develop opportunities in these areas.

— —

CHAPTER 7

Fearless Improvement

"It is about the work we are doing together. We are each wired individually to see things that activate us, but the work of doing what is best for students is what hopefully drives all of us."

Leadership is all about the work we do with others. Throughout the book you have worked with others using the response boxes, tools, inventories, maps, and action steps.

Now what? Throughout the book, we have engaged with some of the most challenging issues in education—issues that require leadership. There is no prescription to solve every issue in every context. I have not provided all of the answers, but I hope I have asked some of the right questions. The good news is that you do not need to solve all of the issues in every context. You also do not have to solve the issues alone. Hopefully, now you see that you cannot. You only need to solve the issues in your context by doing the necessary collective leadership work with others. That is what is happening across this country. Maybe the best news for busy education leaders is the fact that you have already started doing this work if you have read the first six chapters. This is a book about leadership development through doing the necessary work. Therefore, it is fitting that your work so far will drive your work moving forward. The work of schools is always grounded in our students. Take the work you have identified and develop a plan. Then execute the plan.

Now is the time to review some of the tools introduced earlier in the book.

THE FOUR RS REVISITED

In Chapter 2, we examined the Four Rs for schools. When we apply these processes to our own contexts, we begin to see opportunities through reflection and risk. The schools and teachers that shared their stories with us are now part of our personal learning network (PLN) and maybe your school learning network (SLN) if you were able to read about them as a team. Some of the ideas described in previous chapters will not work in your context, some of them will, and some can be adapted. Now is the time to reflect.

Here is some food for thought to consider in your context. These are not easy answers, nor is this entire book distilled to ten recommendations, but it should be good discussion fodder. This is as close as I can come to a list of ideal practices for leadership development.

1. Leadership is about the work. The work dictates the development and who the leaders really are.

2. Collective leadership work requires diverse expertise, not buy-in. Leaders need humility to know what they do not know and the ability to seek the help of others with more expertise.

3. Professional development should include teachers and administrators learning together. The best professional learning impacts practice in schools. This is most likely when the learning opportunity is shared. I hope you are sharing this book.

4. Collective leadership work in schools should be rooted in the classroom. The best administrators long for the classroom and return whenever possible, and the best teacher leaders never lose the perspective of their students.

5. Student outcomes should drive everything. Whenever possible, we should engage students in collective leadership development. Their success is always the focus of any great educator I have ever met—superintendents, principals, or teachers. And it isn't just lip service. You can almost always tell when it is.

Figure 7.1　The Four Rs for Schools

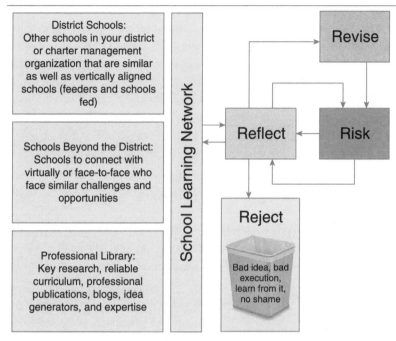

7.1 WHAT CAN WE DO RIGHT NOW?

Review Figure 7.1 and revisit the Box 2.1.

What are three ideas in the book that you can apply right now to make your school better?

What do you think of the five practices listed on the previous page? How many of them are true for your school?

Now revisit your Collective Leadership Map from Chapter 2. What is your adaptive challenge? What are the assets and

(Continued)

(Continued)

barriers your school faces? What might an adaptive solution(s) look like? How will you avoid reductionist technical solutions?

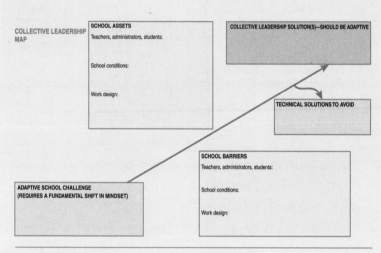

NOTE: A full-scale version of this Collective Leadership Map is available for your use on page 196.

THE COLLECTIVE LEADERSHIP DEVELOPMENT MODEL REVISITED

Each of the previous four chapters was organized around the different components of the Collective Leadership Development Model (See Figure 7.2). This model is theoretical and based on decades of research across sectors. However, it is really meant to be a lens and a mirror. I used the model as a lens to look at three different schools and the experiences of diverse teacher leaders from across the United States. Now you need to use it as a mirror. What do you see when you see your school reflected in this model? Does it accurately reflect what is occurring or are you seeing a funhouse mirror filled with distortions of leadership development efforts gone wrong?

Figure 7.2   Collective Leadership Development Model

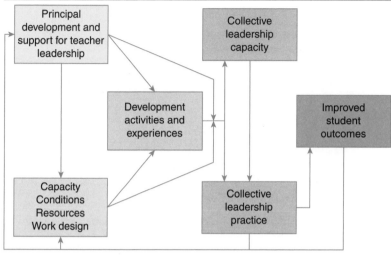

Contexts: Community, District, State, and Federal

7.2 WHAT CAN WE DO RIGHT NOW?

Now that these categories are more than abstract theoretical ideas, what are the components that really need work in your context?

Look back at any of the "What can we do right now?" boxes in Chapters 1 through 6 to remind you of your thinking as you read and discussed other schools and educators. If you are at a rural, urban, or suburban school, maybe spend a little more time reviewing the school chapters most similar to your context.

Complete the model with evidence from your school indicating areas of strength (+) and weakness (-).

(Continued)

(Continued)

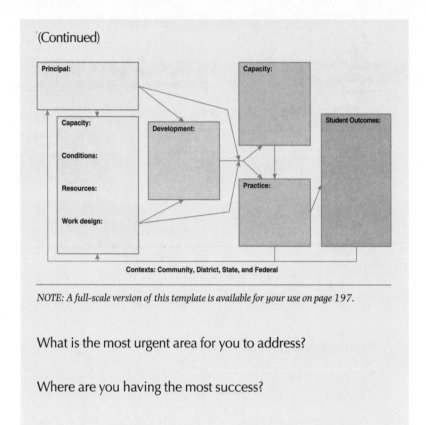

Contexts: Community, District, State, and Federal

NOTE: A full-scale version of this template is available for your use on page 197.

What is the most urgent area for you to address?

Where are you having the most success?

THE "IDEAL" LEADERSHIP DEVELOPMENT MODEL

What is the "ideal" way to complete the leadership development model? Hopefully you realize by now that there are no easy answers for this. Any answer is highly contextualized, and it is impossible to complete a generalized model, but I am going to highlight a few of the things that I believe are ideal for most contexts. Figure 7.3 includes some of the ideal elements based on the leadership development model we proposed.

Ideally, a school is led by a number of catalytic teachers and administrators. This is significantly more likely if principals are catalytic leaders, with a shared vision, and connections to the classroom. These principals have instructional credibility. They conduct walkthroughs, formal observations, or co-teach and

Figure 7.3   Some Ideal Elements for Leadership Development

Principal: Catalyst who supports co-leadership development in support of clearly defined goals and is actively engaged in teaching and learning

Capacity: Established and potential leaders with credibility who see leadership as work
Conditions: Culture and politics that support shared leadership work
Resources: Adequate time, money, and space to support shared leadership work
Work design: Teachers and administrators have time to teach and lead together

Development: Intentional opportunities for teachers and administrators to do work that supports shared goals

Capacity: Teachers and administrators have increased capacity to do the necessary leadership work that leads to improved practice and student outcomes

Practice: Teachers and administrators better support one another through co-led work for improved student outcomes

Student Outcomes:

Increased student satisfaction, attendance, and leadership capacity

Amplified student voices and work through shared leadership

Improved student achievement

Contexts: Community, District, State, and Federal

are not threatened by teacher leadership; in fact, they catalyze it because they know teachers are responsible for the necessary leadership work that is at the core of their shared educational mission.

Capacity, conditions, resources, and work design are really where collective leadership development flourishes or withers. There must be potential leadership capacity among teachers and administrators. This capacity seems to increase when teachers and administrators believe that leadership is about the work that needs to be done. When leaders are not focused on themselves and their own inadequacies, they are more likely to step into leadership work. For this to happen and move to scale, school culture will support diverse leadership work that wide ranges of people undertake with each other. Leadership is most effective when it considers followership, and this is most likely to happen when development opportunities are shared.

Certainly, additional resources are likely to spread or expand the impact of collective leadership development efforts. Intentional leadership development typically requires additional resources. However, in some cases more resources might not be needed to develop leadership. If work is designed in such a way that both administrators and teachers can teach and lead together, then development can occur through this collective leadership work. Hybrid roles that combine teaching and leadership can benefit both teachers and administrators.

Administrators get a foot into the classroom and teachers get a foot out of the classroom. This type of arrangement can be cost neutral. Even in situations where resources are stretched thin, if the leadership work is shared, there does not need to be increased cost. However, if resources of time, money, and human capital are inadequate to meet shared goals, then more money will be necessary.

Sometimes development experiences occur informally as teachers and administrators meet needs that they see. However, development experiences are best when they are intentional because more thought is given to how the work is designed. The following questions are answered when intentional development occurs:

- How will people engage the work?
- How do the development opportunities support the shared goals of the school or district?
- What support is needed for those being developed to be successful?
- What parameters need to be set for the work?

These types of questions increase the likelihood of successful leadership development.

When all of these elements are in place, leadership capacity increases, leadership practice improves, and student outcomes are enhanced. In healthy systems, these improvements inform principal development and the other antecedent elements that affect development.

LEADERSHIP DEVELOPMENT READINESS REVISITED

On the following page is the Leadership Development Readiness (LDR) tool (Figure 7.4) from the second chapter. Hopefully, you are working through this book with a team. Now that you reflected on the schools and leaders, revisit the LDR tool. Fill it out again. Has your team made any progress?

Figure 7.4   LDR Tool

Probe	Teacher	Administrator
1. There is a shared vision of what teacher leadership should look like at our school.	1 2 3 4 5	1 2 3 4 5
2. The principal is comfortable expanding the power of teachers.	1 2 3 4 5	1 2 3 4 5
3. There are teachers who have the ability to work with and help other teachers improve their practice.	1 2 3 4 5	1 2 3 4 5
4. There are teachers who can think through problems well and come up with innovative solutions.	1 2 3 4 5	1 2 3 4 5
5. There is a high degree of trust at our school.	1 2 3 4 5	1 2 3 4 5
6. There is sufficient time for teachers and administrators to develop leadership.	1 2 3 4 5	1 2 3 4 5
7. There are sufficient financial resources for teachers and administrators to develop leadership.	1 2 3 4 5	1 2 3 4 5
8. Administrators and teachers work well together.	1 2 3 4 5	1 2 3 4 5
9. Communication is effective between administrators and teachers.	1 2 3 4 5	1 2 3 4 5
10. Communication is effective between teachers and administrators.	1 2 3 4 5	1 2 3 4 5
11. Our school is a safe place to take risks.	1 2 3 4 5	1 2 3 4 5
12. Teachers at our school are solutions-oriented.	1 2 3 4 5	1 2 3 4 5

(Continued)

(Continued)

13. Administrators at our school are solutions-oriented.	1 2 3 4 5	1 2 3 4 5
14. My work is structured in such a way that I can improve with others.	1 2 3 4 5	1 2 3 4 5
15. Collective leadership development will improve outcomes for students.	1 2 3 4 5	1 2 3 4 5
Total:	_____ /75	_____ /75
Average of all responses (teachers and administrators):	_____ /75	
Difference between teacher and administrator averages:	_____	

7.3 WHAT CAN WE DO RIGHT NOW?

Look at your action steps at the end of Chapter 2 as well as your previous LDR results. How do the scores compare to when you completed this in Chapter 2?

If there has been progress, where has it occurred?

Where is more progress needed?

What kind of feedback loops do you need to determine if your team is progressing toward improved student outcomes?

ACCELERATING YOUR WORK TOGETHER

I have yet to come across a school that does not believe leadership needs to be developed. A recent report from RAND demonstrates the importance of leadership development, specifically in the context of the Every Student Succeeds Act's (ESSA) evidence tiers (Herman et al., 2016). Now is the time to take advantage of the increased flexibility available to states, districts, and schools—particularly the flexibility that is found in the evidence tiers. Now is the time to become catalysts—change agents who accelerate the work and know that it is not about them. Below is a brief summary of the findings from the report:

- School leadership can be a powerful driver of improved education outcomes.
- Activities designed to improve school leadership demonstrate positive impact on student, teacher, and principal outcomes, based on research that is consistent with ESSA evidence tiers.
- ESSA expands opportunities for states and districts to use federal funding for initiatives that strive to improve the quality of school leaders.
- ESSA's evidence tiers provide a framework for using evidence in school leadership policy and practice.
- ESSA provides some flexibility for states to interpret and apply evidence requirements.

Possibilities for funding for leadership development in ESSA exist in the following places:

Title I, Section 1114 (p. 69): Schoolwide Programs

Title II, Section 2101 (pp. 159–166): State Activities

Title II, Section 2103 (pp. 168–172): Local Use of Funds

Title II, Section 2211–2213 (pp. 173–178): Teacher and School Leader Incentive Program (formerly the Teacher Incentive Fund)

Title II, Section 2243 (pp. 192–194): School Leader Recruitment and Supports

Because resources are always scarce and your time is valuable, I did a review of the entire ESSA to determine where money might be available for leadership development (See Sidebar).

What should drive the answers that schools might find through this increased flexibility? While some argue that there are benefits to the 30,000 foot view that federal policymakers use to "see like a state," (Ravitch, 2010) I see positive change coming from a different direction. Those people who are closest to teaching and learning have to be the innovators, and then district, state, and federal policy should support those positive innovations. In theory, this is what ESSA should do. Teacher leaders' classroom practice affords them the perspective relationships necessary for instructional leadership (Lai & Cheung, 2015; Mangin & Stoelinga, 2010). When leadership work is determined by those doing the teaching and learning, positive change is more likely to occur (See Figure 7.5).

Even if policymakers might disagree, they cannot refute the fact that change will not happen if teachers, students, and building administrators are not invested. We cannot, nor should we attempt to, work around them.

Working *With* Instead of *Around* Administrators

Federal, state, and local policymakers should work with building administrators to understand school-level challenges. This should go without saying. However, teachers also need to work with, not around, building administrators. Part of working with them is not separating teachers and administrators into different camps. We all need to think of ourselves as possible catalysts for improvement that results in improved outcomes—not

Figure 7.5   Grassroots Leadership and Positive Change

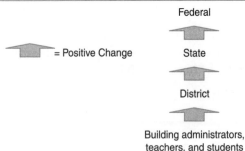

necessarily for us—but for students. The good news is that oftentimes what is best for teachers and administrators is best for students. Most of the time, advocating "for students" means advocating "for the adults in the building" who serve them. Let's move past these false dichotomies of who is for kids and who is against kids. We need to start with the assumption that we are all on the same team.

The job of the comprehensive high school principal may be the toughest job in education. The principals I interviewed are at everything—games, concerts, club events, art shows, plays—and they are tweeting about everything they see. Being a principal can be lonely, anxiety inducing, and sleep reducing (Holmes, 2016). The administrators I interviewed and worked with want and need to share leadership. Some of them were great teachers before they were administrators and know that their role is primarily to support the relationships between teachers and students.

Teachers who move into administration or other school support roles often struggle with defining their leadership. When do I stop being a teacher and become an administrator? When do I become a sellout to the teaching profession? To use a *Star Wars* metaphor, it is almost as if leadership beyond the classroom means crossing over to the dark side. One teacher leader in North Carolina articulated her struggle this way:

> That is why I think I struggle with teacher leadership—if I don't have students, can I still be a teacher leader? If I don't have students right at this moment, can I still recognize the needs of students and what needs to be done to get that done in a way that is helpful? I think there is a teacher leadership spirit.

This sentiment is indicative of the divide teachers see between themselves and administrators. We certainly need to blur the lines so that shared goals and missions dictate the work that is done, and we need to stop seeing each other through positional lenses. We all have different roles and responsibilities, but the work should determine who leads and when. This is the point of collective leadership. For teachers and administrators, the work is so much harder when they have to work around other people instead of sharing the load. Working with each other is more than liking each other. Working together means asking hard questions, understanding as much as being understood, and saying "no" sometimes, but most of the time it is about making it easy to say "yes." Most of all it is about trust and respect.

One of the best ways I have seen to build trust and understanding is to work together toward shared goals. This is just another reason to consider leadership as work.

> *Working with each other is more than liking each other. Working together means asking hard questions, understanding as much as being understood, and saying "no" sometimes, but most of the time it is about making it easy to say "yes." Most of all it is about trust and respect.*

Working *With* Instead of *Around* Teachers

Administrators are also responsible for building this bridge. Without teachers' leadership, administrators will not be successful (Spillane, Diamond, & Jita, 2003) in the short term, and certainly not in the long term (Danielson, 2007). The administrators profiled in this book prioritized relationships, trust, and space for teachers to lead. The teacher leaders I interviewed cited these characteristics as vital. When we do not have relational trust or space for work, we begin to see others as obstacles to what we want to get done. This does not serve any of us well.

When people advocate for hybrid roles, they often think of teachers stepping into pseudo-administrative roles while keeping a foot in the classroom. I always find it interesting that we do not think of administrators stepping into hybrid roles. Why not? At many independent schools, administrators teach a class a day. Why is that so impractical for public school administrators? For those administrators who truly love the classroom, why not figure out a way to go back to it on a regular basis? Even if this is just in a co-teaching role, this reentry to the classroom can go a long way toward reminding us of the challenges and joys that teachers and students experience on a daily basis.

Although I was moving into a far different role than an administrator, a few years ago I stepped into higher education and teacher preparation. At times, teacher preparation is accused of being disconnected from real teachers and teaching. Being cognizant of that, and recognizing that I would enjoy teaching college students, but miss kids, I asked in my interview if I would be able to keep returning to K-12 classrooms to teach. I was told in the interview, "You may have to give that up. The rigors of teaching, research, and institutional service will probably take up your time." To see teaching in K-12 classrooms as being outside the role of a teacher preparation provider was troubling to me, and despite the bleak prediction I have managed to get into elementary classrooms to teach each year.

Administrators face a similar predicament. Their work is seen as too demanding to carve out time to get back to teaching. However, by working with teachers who can take on some aspects of leadership and administrative work, they can carve out time to get into classrooms.

When administrators step back into the classroom, it develops a level of instructional credibility from teachers. Teachers who reported that their administrators knew what was going on in their classrooms also reported higher levels of administrator support in general. How much stronger could that bond be if teachers saw principals as instructional experts, not because of something they read and shared, but because of shared teaching practice? Yes, this is vulnerable, but vulnerability is necessary for the development of trust. This can lead to the kind of disruptive engagement education needs.

Working *With* Instead of *Around* Students and Parents

What if we took disruptive engagement a step or two further? What if we continued to bring students into the school improvement process in a manner similar to the rural high school? What if parents were a part of a team committed to improving the climate of a school as they were at the urban school? What if students co-designed curriculum, co-taught (Emdin, 2016), or shared successes at staff meetings? These are all things that are already happening. Teachers and administrators across the country are leading with their students. From social justice causes, to literary magazines, to Club 9, to stoichiometry calculators, leaders are changing the trajectories of their communities. These leaders include students and parents. Their efforts are catalyzed when administrators, teachers, and paraprofessionals all work alongside each other.

As is the case with all leadership work, there are some tasks that have to be done by particular people with certain positions.

For example, second-grade students do not need to be involved in developing compensation policies for teachers. However, there are many instances where there is more expertise in a community than is currently tapped. If we truly want to transform schools, reaching out more, not less, is probably in order.

Improving schools is challenging. What the urban high school went through with the firing of all of the administrators does not always lead to success. In fact, the U.S. Department of Education made a $7 billion bet through School Improvement Grants and found no effect on student learning (Dragoset et al., 2017). This makes progress in these kinds of challenging environments that much more impressive. The question is: How can we progress faster?

FEARLESS IMPROVEMENT

The first thing to remember is that collective leadership work is not about you. This fact is freeing, if you can embrace it. You do not need a particular title, personality type, or level of charisma. You just need to identify the work that needs to be done to reach shared goals and begin doing that work with others. Obviously, intentional development efforts are helpful, but most development actually occurs as we work with others. If you embrace the notion that leadership work is not about you, humility increases, and defensiveness decreases. You no longer need to protect territory or feel that your identity is wrapped up in the success or failure of some initiative. You can rely on others—others with the expertise to make the work successful. When you start doing this, then your learning networks—both personal and school—become very important.

> *If you embrace the notion that leadership work is not about you, humility increases, and defensiveness decreases.*

Personal and School Learning Networks

Learning networks should improve your work. They should also make your life easier. In twenty-one years in education, I have not encountered any challenges that are completely unique to me. Someone, somewhere, has dealt with the issue. The same is true for the schools where I worked and the schools that I studied.

While each school is unique when every variable is considered, other schools have addressed similar challenges. The key is to tap into the expertise those schools already developed in order to find solutions that can work for your school.

Networked Improvement Communities

The Carnegie Foundation (Bryk, Gomez, Grunow, & LeMahieu, 2015) is focusing its efforts on Networked Improvement

7.4 WHAT CAN WE DO RIGHT NOW?

Go back to your Collective Leadership Map in Box 7.1.

- What challenge did you identify?

- What leadership development did you identify?

- What resources (research, evidence, thought pieces) can help solve this challenge?

- What people can help you solve this challenge (think PLN)?

- What other schools might have insights or possible solutions (think SLN)?

- For your PLN or SLN, be sure to address the following:
  - How will you connect with the necessary people?
  - Who will connect with them?
  - When will they report back their findings?

Communities (NICs). They are attempting to help schools build on what has been learned in the improvement sciences. The first thing to do is to identify a problem of practice, which is something you have already done. Then you develop a theory of practice improvement. This theory of practice is developed and tracked using improvement research methods (methods that allow you to capture growth over time). This type of assessment requires the development of infrastructure that allows you to determine progress. This is something that would occur across schools in an NIC. In order for this "learning by doing" to occur, you must attend to cultural norms that are consistent with the shared goals of the NIC. This requires transparency and unblinking attention on where you really are as a school, both at the beginning of the process and along the way.

Contextualized Tools

There are many tools available for you to do this work. The Carnegie Foundation has many tools (https://www.carnegie-foundation.org) to help support your work as an NIC. Several other organizations have tools in place to support the leadership

7.5 WHAT CAN WE DO RIGHT NOW?

What is a shared problem of practice for your school and at least one other (See Box 7.4)?

- What is our school's theory of practice improvement?

- How will we assess improvement?

- What infrastructure will we need to assess that improvement?

work of teachers and administrators. For example, the Center for Teaching Quality (CTQ) is developing a suite of tools to help tell leadership stories that can provide evidence of impact to scale-up work (http://www.teachingquality.org/supports-services). These tools help individuals reflect on their leadership work with students, colleagues, and their communities. The Center for Creative Leadership (https://www.ccl.org) also has tools for leadership development.

This list is far from comprehensive, but there are organizations that see leadership as something far more impactful than a position. They want to scale up that work so that more students are better served. Through your PLN or SLN, you can identify resources. Only use the ones that work for you.

7.6 WHAT CAN WE DO RIGHT NOW?

On a scale of 1 to 10, how close are you to being part of an NIC?

1 = "We exist on an island of expertise. We cannot learn anything from anyone else."

10 = "We are already part of an intercontinental NIC of expert educators."

| 1 | 2 | 3 | 4 | 5 | 6 | 7 | 8 | 9 | 10 |

What tools do you need to develop leadership at your school?

Are any of these already available in your district, state, or through an organization?

Who could be a part of your NIC?

How could you overcome the obstacles to becoming an NIC or accelerate your work as an NIC?

POLICYMAKERS, DO NO HARM

I hope that policymakers at the local, state, and federal levels read this book. I hope their first impulse is to support the good work that is happening in schools, and at a minimum avoid harming that work. Their expertise can be valuable as part of a PLN or SLN. However, their value is in supporting the efforts already occurring in schools. This seems to be the motivation of ESSA from the federal level, as authority seems to be shifting back to the states. I hope this movement extends to the local levels as well.

The innovative work described throughout this book is already happening in schools, in rural, urban, and suburban schools across the country. Policies should support this work, not constrain it, or construct impediments in the form of onerous paperwork or bureaucratic requirements. The further removed we are from students, the more we need to listen, observe, and learn. Good policy should be grounded in good practice.

> *The further removed we are from students, the more we need to listen, observe, and learn.*

"YES" AND "NO"

We started with the mint officer as a poor example of leadership development. In between the mint officer and the final pages of the book, I have tried to provide numerous examples that move us well beyond the mint officer to real collective leadership. We need to say "no" to attempts to appoint more mint officers because this is not real leadership, and it does not benefit students beyond having teachers with slightly fresher breath.

Beyond egregious examples that we should obviously resist, we also have to learn to say "no" to things that might be good, but do not serve the shared goals of our schools. Teachers and administrators get spread thin because of their diverse expertise and their inability to say "no." Teachers see so many needs in the classroom, and they want to fix them all. We need each other to help us say "no" in order to balance our idealism with reality. Gritty optimism has to replace naïve idealism. Gritty optimism requires us to say "no" to things that do not produce results for our students. Gritty optimism requires us to say "no" to things that render us ineffective because we can no longer perform all the tasks required of us. We must let the work dictate our response. We need to ask: What can we actually accomplish? Not: What do we hope we can accomplish if we had twenty-six hours in a day or only slept two hours a night?

At the other end of the response spectrum, we need to learn to make it easy for others to say "yes" to the work that matters most. Sometimes this means we need to say "yes" to other people's ideas. One of my pet peeves about teacher hero books and movies is that every idea that the hero pushes is always his or her own. The teacher is always fighting the system or showing other less caring, less skilled teachers what it really takes to be inspirational. When does the hero support another teacher's idea? What about supporting an administrator who is also trying to drive positive change?

Most of the time, making it easy to say "yes" means being able to see a challenge from someone else's perspective. Teachers need to be able to understand the different pressures on building administrators—parents, budgets, paperwork, central office matters, other teachers, legal issues, students, school boards, and local, state, and federal policies. Building administrators need to be able to understand the different pressures on teachers—the immediate needs of students, parents, testing, paperwork, grading, individualized education plans, and the many policies that dictate what occurs in a classroom. Both teachers and building administrators need to understand the challenges of central office administrators—politics, school boards, budgets, legal issues, curriculum, assessments, personnel decisions, technology, and local, state, and federal policies. Sadly, these lists of pressures are not comprehensive.

If we want others to support the work that needs to be done, we have to frame that work in such a way that all they have to do is to say "yes." Administrators shoot down many ideas from teachers because teachers do not have a way to pay for it. Teachers shoot down many ideas from administrators because the ideas do not fit their classroom contexts. Repeatedly in my interviews, school administrators and teachers felt constrained by their central offices. This does not have to be the case. If we can step up to do the leadership work, and step back when it comes to taking credit, we will see that this work has to be done together. I know there are more stories of catalytic teachers and administrators out there. Let's get to work.

Chapter Review: What Matters Most for Schools (and in This Chapter)?

❖ Leadership is about the work. The work of schools is always grounded in our students. Take the work you have identified and develop a plan. Then execute the plan.

❖ All elements, especially the feedback loops, of the Collective Leadership Development Model must be considered.

❖ Federal policies like ESSA can provide opportunities for collective leadership development.

❖ When leadership work is determined by those doing the teaching and learning, positive change is more likely to occur.

❖ Teachers and administrators should work with, instead of around, each other.

❖ Teachers and administrators should work with, instead of around, students and parents.

❖ Fearless improvement means embracing collective leadership as work. This increases humility and decreases defensiveness.

❖ Schools are more likely to improve when they are in networks that collect and share data transparently.

❖ Policymakers must avoid harming school improvement efforts.

❖ Know when to say "no." Know how to make it easy for others to say "yes."

Action Steps

After completing this book, you should have identified plenty of opportunities.

For Administrators and Teachers

1. Based on your work in this book, identify one thing you will say "no" to.

2. Based on your work in this book, identify one thing that you will make it easy for someone else to say "yes" to.

3. Describe how these two actions will support a shared goal of your school.

4. Based on your work in this book, identify one thing your school will say "no" to.

5. Based on your work in this book, identify one thing that your school will make it easy for someone else to say "yes" to.

6. Describe how these two actions will support a shared goal of your school.

7. Track your progress and be transparent with other schools in your network.

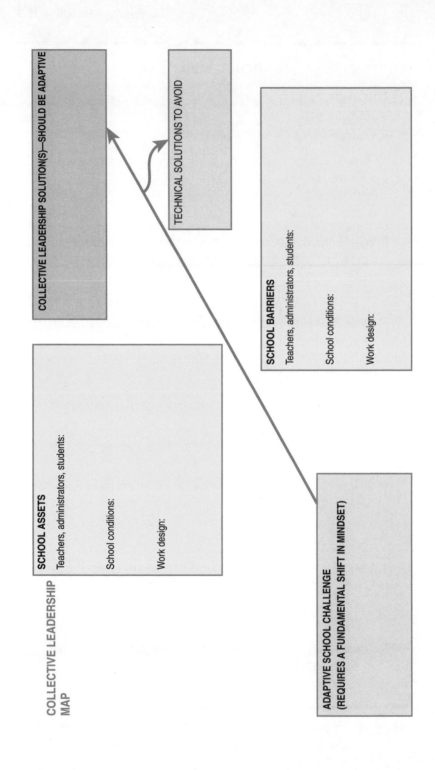

COLLECTIVE LEADERSHIP MAP

COLLECTIVE LEADERSHIP SOLUTION(S)—SHOULD BE ADAPTIVE

TECHNICAL SOLUTIONS TO AVOID

SCHOOL ASSETS

Teachers, administrators, students:

School conditions:

Work design:

SCHOOL BARRIERS

Teachers, administrators, students:

School conditions:

Work design:

ADAPTIVE SCHOOL CHALLENGE
(REQUIRES A FUNDAMENTAL SHIFT IN MINDSET)

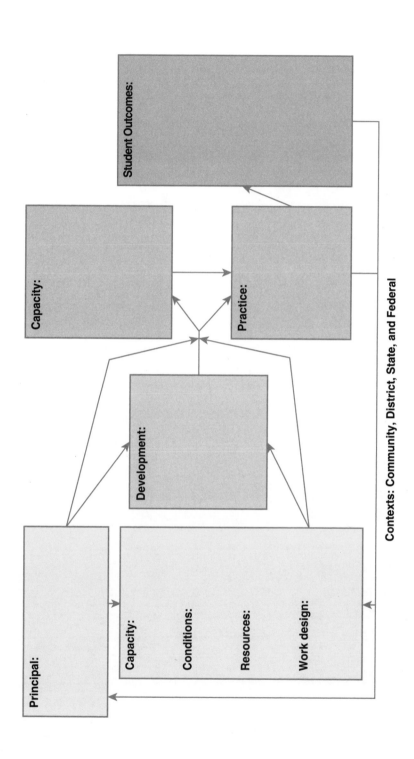

Contexts: Community, District, State, and Federal

References

Aldrich, H., & Herker, D. (1977). Boundary spanning roles and organizational structure. *Academy of Management Review, 2*(2), 217–230.

Avolio, B. J. (2010). *Full range leadership development* (2nd ed.). Thousand Oaks, CA: SAGE.

Branch, G., Hanushek, E. A., & Rivkin, S. G. (2012). *Estimating the effect of leaders on public sector productivity: The case of school principals* (No. 17803). National Bureau of Economic Research. Retrieved from http://www.nber.org/papers/w17803

Bransford, J., Brown, A. L., Cocking, R. R., & National Research Council. (2000). *How people learn: Brain, mind, experience, and school* (Expanded edition). Washington, DC: National Academy Press.

Brown, B. (2012). *Daring greatly: How the courage to be vulnerable transforms the way we live, love, parent, and lead.* New York, NY: Avery.

Bryk, A., & Schneider, B. (2002). *Trust in schools: A core resource for improvement.* New York, NY: Russell Sage Foundation.

Bryk, A. S., Gomez, L. M., Grunow, A., & LeMahieu, P. G. (2015). *Learning to improve: How America's schools can get better at getting better.* Cambridge, MA: Harvard Education Press.

Burke, W. W. (2014). *Organizational change: Theory and practice* (4th ed.). Los Angeles, CA: SAGE.

Campion, M. A., Mumford, T. V., Morgeson, F. P., & Nahrgang, J. D. (2005). Work redesign: Eight obstacles and opportunities. *Human Resource Management, 44*(4), 367–390.

Collins, J. (2001). *Good to great: Why some companies make the leap... and others don't.* New York, NY: Harper Collins.

Collins, J., & Hansen, M. T. (2011). *Great by choice: Uncertainty, chaos, and luck–why some thrive despite them all.* New York, NY: Harper Collins.

Conger, J. (1992). *Learning to lead: The art of transforming managers into leaders*. San Francisco, CA: Jossey-Bass.

Curtis, R. (2013). *Finding a new way: Leveraging teacher leadership to meet unprecedented demands*. Washington, DC: The Aspen Institute.

Danielson, C. (2007). The many faces of leadership. *Educational Leadership, 65*(1), 14–19.

Darling-Hammond, L., Bransford, J., LePage, P., Hammerness, K., & Duffy, H. (Eds.). (2005). *Preparing teachers for a changing world: What teachers should learn and be able to do*. San Francisco, CA: Jossey-Bass.

Darling-Hammond, L., Wei, R. C., Andree, A., Richardson, N., & Orphanos, S. (2009). *Professional learning in the learning profession: A status report on teacher development in the United States and abroad*. Washington, DC: National Staff Development Council. Retrieved from http://www.learningforward.org/docs/pdf/nsdcstudy2009.pdf

Day, C., Gu, Q., & Sammons, P. (2016). The impact of leadership on student outcomes. *Educational Administration Quarterly, 52*(2), 221–258. Retrieved from https://doi.org/10.1177/0013161X15616863

Day, D. V., Zaccaro, S. J., & Halpin, S. M. (2004). *Leadership development for transforming organizations: Growing leaders for tomorrow*. New York, NY: Psychology Press.

Deming, W. E. (1993). *Deming four-day seminar*. Phoenix, AZ. Retrieved from https://blog.deming.org/2015/02/a-bad-system-will-beat-a-good-person-every-time/

Donohoo, J., & Velasco, M. (2016). *The transformative power of collaborative inquiry: Realizing change in schools and classrooms*. Thousand Oaks, CA: Corwin.

Dragoset, L., Herrmann, M., Deke, J., James-Burdumy, S., Gaczewski, C., Boyle, A., ... Giffin, J. (2017). *School improvement grants: Implementation and effectiveness* (No. NCEE 2017–4013). Washington, DC: National Center for Education Evaluation and Regional Assistance, Institute of Education Science, U.S. Department of Education. Retrieved from https://ies.ed.gov/ncee/pubs/20174013/pdf/20174013.pdf

Duckworth, A. (2016). *Grit: The power of passion and perseverance*. New York, NY: Scribner.

Duke, D. (2008). *How do you turn around a low-performing school?* Paper presented at the ASCD Annual Conference, New Orleans, LA.

Duncan, A. (2014). *Teach to lead: Advancing teacher leadership* [oral presentation]. Teaching and Learning Conference in Washington, D.C. by the U.S. Department of Education. Retrieved from http://www.ed.gov/news/speeches/teach-lead-advancing-teacher-leadership

Durand, F. T., Lawson, H. A., Wilcox, K. C., & Schiller, K. S. (2016). The role of district office leaders in the adoption and implementation of the Common Core State Standards in elementary schools. *Educational Administration Quarterly, 52*(1), 45–74.

Eckert, J. (2016). *The novice advantage: Fearless practice for every teacher.* Thousand Oaks, CA: Corwin.

Eckert, J., Ulmer, J., Khatchatryan, E., & Ledesma, P. (2016). Career pathways of teacher leaders: Adding and path-finding new professional roles. *Professional Development in Education, 42*(5), 687–709.

Emdin, C. (2016). *For white folks who teach in the hood and the rest of y'all too: Reality pedagogy and urban education.* Boston, MA: Beacon Press.

Ericsson, K. A., Krampe, R. T., & Tesch-Romer, C. (1993). The role of deliberate practice in the acquisition of expert performance. *Psychological Review, 100*(3), 363–406.

Ernst, C., & Chroot-Mason, D. (2010). *Boundary spanning leadership: Six practices for solving problems, driving innovation, and transforming organizations.* New York, NY: McGraw Hill.

Firestone, W. A. (1996). Leadership: Roles or functions? In K. Leithwood, J. Chapman, D. Corson, P. Hallinger, & A. Hart (Eds.), *International handbook of educational leadership and administration, Part I* (pp. 395–418). Boston, MA: Kluwer.

Fulmer, R. M. (1997). The evolving paradigm of leadership development. *Organizational Dynamics, 25*(5), 59–72.

Goldring, E. (1997). Educational leadership: Schools, environments, and boundary spanning. In *Educational management: Strategy, quality, and resources.* Philadelphia, PA: Open University Press.

Goldstein, D. (2014). *The teacher wars: A history of America's most embattled profession.* New York, NY: Doubleday.

Grissom, J. A., Kalogrides, K., & Loeb, S. (2015). Using student test scores to measure principal performance. *Education Evaluation and Policy Analysis, 37*(1), 3–28.

Hackman, J. R., & Oldham, G. R. (1980). *Work redesign.* Reading, MA: Addison-Wesley.

Hanushek, E. (1992). The trade-off between child quantity and quality. *Journal of Political Economy, 100*(1), 84–117.

Hargreaves, A., & Fullan, M. (2012). *Professional capital: Transforming teaching in every school.* New York, NY: Teachers College Press.

Hattie, J. (2009). *Visible learning: A synthesis of over 800 meta-analyses relating to achievement.* New York, NY: Routledge.

Hattie, J. (2012). *Visible learning for teachers: Maximizing impact on learning.* New York, NY: Routledge.

Hattie, J. (2015). *What works best in education: The politics of collaborative expertise* (Open Ideas). London, UK: Pearson. Retrieved from https://www.pearson.com/content/dam/corporate/global/pearson-dot-com/files/hattie/150526_ExpertiseWEB_V1.pdf

Hattie, J., & Yates, G. (2014). *Visible learning and the science of how we learn.* New York, NY: Routledge.

Heifetz, R. (1998). *Leadership without easy answers.* Cambridge, MA: Harvard University Press.

Herman, R., Gates, S. M., Arifkhanova, A., Bega, A., Chavez-Herrerias, E. R., Han, E., ... Wrabel, S. (2016). *School leadership interventions under the Every Student Succeeds Act: Evidence review.* RAND Corporation. Retrieved from http://www.ccssoessaguide.org/wp-content/uploads/2016/12/down_rr-1550-1_12-5-2016.pdf

Hess, F. M. (2015). *The cage-busting teacher.* Cambridge, MA: Harvard Education Press.

Hiebert, J., & Stigler, J. W. (2017). Teaching versus teachers as a lever for change: Comparing a Japanese and a U.S. perspective on improving instruction. *Educational Researcher, 46*(4), 169–176. Retrieved from https://doi.org/10.3102/0013189X17711899

Holmes, D. (2016). The inner life of school leaders. *Independent School, 76*(1), 52–56.

Humphrey, S. E., Nahrgang, J. D., & Morgeson, F. P. (2007). Integrating motivational, social, and contextual work design features: A meta-analytic summary and theoretical extension of the work design literature. *Journal of Applied Psychology, 92*(5), 1332–1356.

Illinois State Board of Education. (2016). *Illinois school report card.* Retrieved from http://illinoisreportcard.com/Default.aspx

Jackson, C. K., & Bruegmann, E. (2009). *Teaching students and teaching each other: The importance of peer learning for teachers* (No. NBER Working Paper 15202). Cambridge, MA: National Bureau of Economic Research. Retrieved from www.nber.org/papers/w15202

Jensen, B., Roberts-Hull, K., Magee, J., & Ginnivan, L. (2016). *Not so elementary: Primary school teacher quality in high-performing systems.* Washington, DC: National Center on Education and the Economy.

Jensen, B., Sonnemann, J., Roberts-Hull, K., & Hunter, A. (2016). *Beyond PD: Teacher professional learning in high-performing systems.* Washington, DC: National Center on Education and the Economy. Retrieved from http://www.ncee.org/wp-content/uploads/2015/08/BeyondPDWeb.pdf

Katzenmeyer, K., & Moller, G. (2009). *Awakening the sleeping giant: Helping teacher leaders develop as leaders* (3rd ed.). Thousand Oaks, CA: Corwin.

Kellerman, B. (2004). *Bad leadership: What it is, how it happens, why it matters.* Boston, MA: Harvard Business School Press.

Kraft, M. A., & Papay, J. P. (2016). *Developing workplaces where teachers stay, improve, and succeed.* Washington, DC: The Albert Shanker Institute. Retrieved from http://distributedleadership.org/assets/asi-(2016).pdf

Lai, E., & Cheung, D. (2015). Enacting teacher leadership: The role of teachers in bringing about change. *Educational Management Administration & Leadership, 43*(5), 673–692. Retrieved from https://doi.org/10.1177/1741143214535742

Leithwood, K., & Mascall, B. (2008). Collective leadership effects on student achievement. *Educational Administration Quarterly, 44*(4), 529–561.

Leithwood, K., Seashore-Louis, K., Anderson, S., & Wahlstrom, K. (2004). *How leadership influences student learning.* New York, NY: The Wallace Foundation.

Lencioni, P. (2002). *The five dysfunctions of a team: A leadership fable.* San Francisco, CA: Jossey-Bass.

Lencioni, P. (2016). *The ideal team player: How to cultivate and recognize the three essential virtues.* San Francisco, CA: Jossey-Bass.

Lieberman, A., & Miller, L. (2004). *Teacher leadership.* San Francisco, CA: Jossey-Bass.

Mangin, M. M., & Stoelinga, S. R. (2008). *Effective teacher leadership: Using research to inform and reform.* New York, NY: Teachers College Press.

Mangin, M., & Stoelinga, S. R. (2010). The future of instructional teacher leader roles. *Education Forum, 74*(1), 49–62.

McCullough, D. (2015). *The Wright brothers.* New York, NY: Simon & Shuster.

MetLife. (2013). *The MetLife survey of the American teacher: Challenges for school leadership.* New York, NY: Author. Retrieved from https://www.metlife.com/assets/cao/foundation/MetLife-Teacher-Survey-2012.pdf

Murphy, J. (2005). *Connecting teacher leadership and school improvement.* Thousand Oaks, CA: Corwin.

Pennington, K. (2013). *The landscape of today's teachers shaping policy.* Washington, DC: The Center for American Progress.

Pollan, M. (2013). *Cooked: A natural history of transformation.* New York, NY: Penguin Press.

Ravitch, D. (2010). *The death and life of the great American school system: How testing and choice are undermining education.* New York, NY: Basic Books.

Rivkin, S. G., Hanushek, E. A., & Kain, J. F. (2005). Teachers, schools, and academic achievement. *Econometrica, 73*(2), 417–458.

Ronfeldt, M., Farmer, S. O., McQueen, K., & Grissom, J. A. (2015). Teacher collaboration in instructional teams and student achievement. *American Educational Research Journal, 52*(3), 475–514.

Rozovsky, J. (2015, November 17). *The five keys to a successful Google team.* Retrieved from https://rework.withgoogle.com/blog/five-keys-to-a-successful-google-team/

Sanders, W. L., & Rivers, J. C. (1996). *Cumulative and residual effects of teachers on future student academic achievement: Research progress report.* Knoxville, TN: University of Tennessee Value-Added Research and Assessment Center.

School Leaders Network. (2014). *Churn: The high cost of principal turnover.* Retrieved from http://connectleadsucceed.org/sites/default/files/principal_turnover_cost.pdf

Seashore-Louis, K., Leithwood, K., Wahlstrom, K., & Anderson, S. (2010). *Learning for leadership: Investigating the links to improved student learning.* Alexandria, VA: Educational Research.

Smylie, M. A., Conley, S., & Marks, H. M. (2002). Exploring new approaches to teacher leadership for school improvement. In J. Murphy (Ed.), *The educational leadership challenge: Redefining leadership for the 21st century. 101st Yearbook of the National Society for the Study of Education, Part I* (pp. 162–188). Chicago, IL: National Society for the Study of Education.

Smylie, M. A., & Denny, J. W. (1990). Teacher leadership: Tensions and ambiguities in organizational perspective. *Educational Administration Quarterly, 26*(3), 235–259.

Smylie, M. A., & Eckert, J. (2017). Beyond superheroes and advocacy: The pathway of teacher leadership development. *Educational Management Administration & Leadership,* 1–22. Retrieved from https://doi.org/10.1177/1741143217684893

Smylie, M. A., & Mayoretz, D. (2009). Footnotes to teacher leadership. In L. J. Saha & A. G. Dworkin (Eds.), *International handbook of research on teachers and teaching* (Vol. 21, pp. 277–289). New York, NY: Springer.

Spillane, J. P., Diamond, J. B., & Jita, L. (2003). Leading instruction: The distribution of leadership for instruction. *Journal of Curriculum Studies, 35*(5), 533–543. Retrieved from https://doi.org/10.1080/0022027021000041972

Szczesiul, S. A., & Huizenga, J. R. (2015). Bridging structure and agency: Exploring the riddle of teacher leadership in teacher collaboration. *Journal of School Leadership, 25*(2), 368–410.

University of Chicago. (2016). *5Essentials.* Retrieved from https://illinois.5-essentials.org/2016/

Van Velsor, E., McCauley, C. D., & Ruderman, M. N. (Eds.). (2010). *The center for creative leadership handbook of leadership development* (3rd ed.). San Francisco, CA: Jossey-Bass.

Wenner, J. A., & Campbell, T. (2017). The theoretical and empirical basis of teacher leadership: A review of the literature. *Review of Educational Research, 87*(1), 134–171. Retrieved from https://doi.org/10.3102/0034654316653478

Willingham, D. T. (2009). *Why don't students like school?* San Francisco, CA: Jossey-Bass.

Woolley, A. W., Chabris, C. F., Pentland, A., Hashmi, N., & Malone, T. W. (2010). Evidence for a collective intelligence factor in the performance of human groups. *Science, 330*(6004), 686. Retrieved from https://doi.org/10.1126/science.1193147

Wright, A. (2016). *How principals can support teacher leaders: Lessons from Glenn O. Swing Elementary School.* Retrieved from http://www.teachingquality.org/content/blogs/barnett-berry/how-principals-can-support-teacher-leaders-lessons-glenn-o-swing

York-Barr, J., & Duke, D. (2004). What do we know about teacher leadership? Findings from two decades of scholarship. *Review of Educational Research, 74*(3), 255–316.

Yukl, G. (2013). *Leadership in organizations* (8th ed.). Boston, MA: Pearson.

Index

A SAGE Publishing Company

Helping educators make the greatest impact

CORWIN HAS ONE MISSION: to enhance education through intentional professional learning.

We build long-term relationships with our authors, educators, clients, and associations who partner with us to develop and continuously improve the best evidence-based practices that establish and support lifelong learning.